HAL LEONARD ORGAN ADVENTURE SERIES

105
FAVORITE HYMNS

arranged by Bill Irwin

T0045406

CONTENTS

NOTE: A Registration Number appears above each song arrangement. Before playing each song, locate that number on the Registration Chart in the back of this book and set up the organ voices and controls as indicated.

HAL•LEONARD®
CORPORATION
7777 W. BLUEMOUND RD. P.O. BOX 13819 MILWAUKEE, WI 53213

Sweet Hour Of Prayer

Registration 17

Words by William W. Walford
Music by William B. Bradbury

Moderately slow

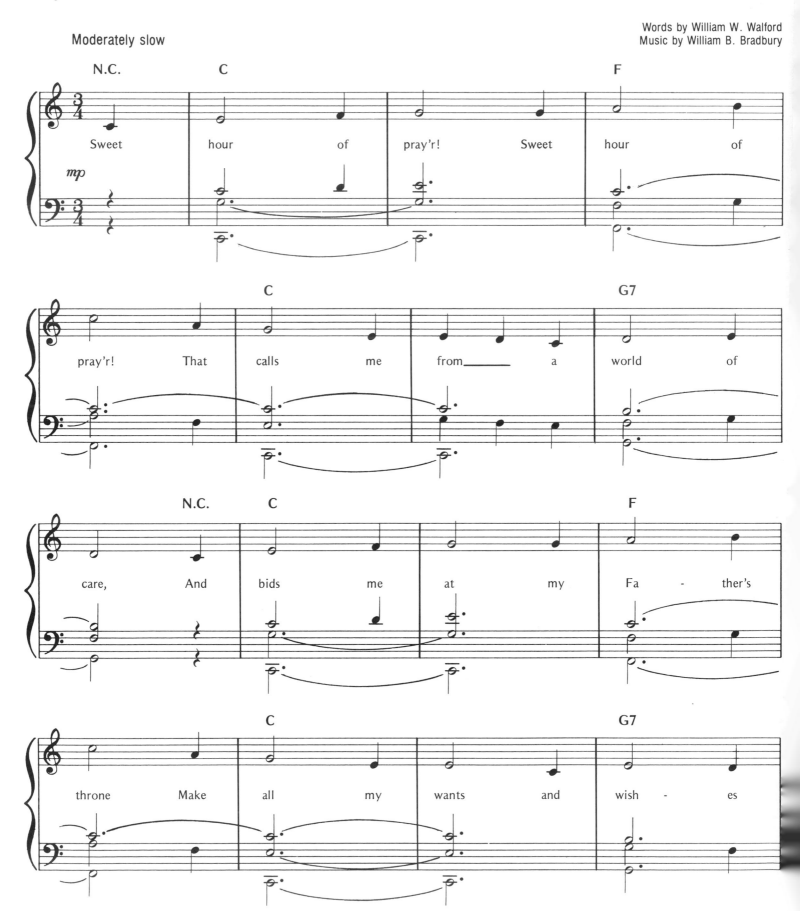

Sweet hour of pray'r! Sweet hour of pray'r! That calls me from a world of care, And bids me at my Fa - ther's throne Make all my wants and wish - es

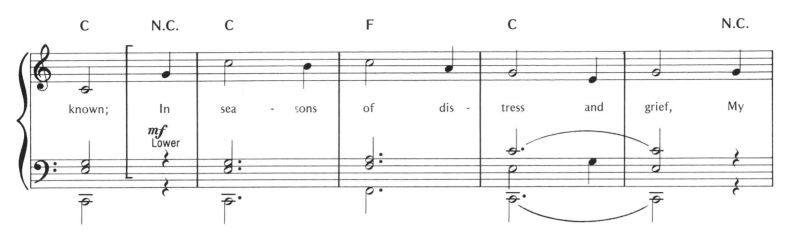

known; In sea - sons of dis - tress and grief, My

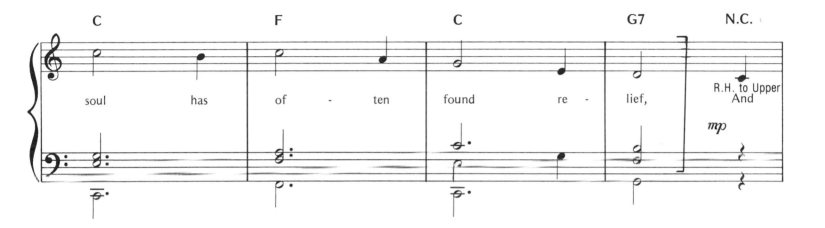

soul has of - ten found re - lief, And

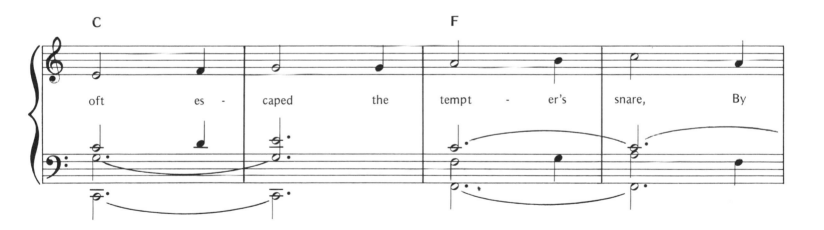

oft es - caped the tempt - er's snare, By

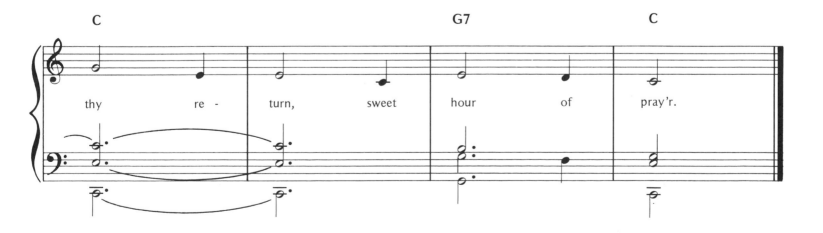

thy re - turn, sweet hour of pray'r.

The Church In The Wildwood

Registration 12

Words and Music by
William S. Pitts

Just As I Am

Registration 15

Words by William B. Bradbury
Music by Charlotte Elliot

Onward, Christian Soldiers

Registration 10

Words by Sabine Baring-Gould
Music by Arthur S. Sullivan

Majestically

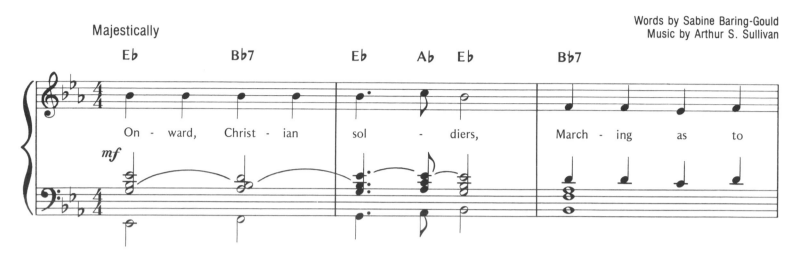

On - ward, Christ - ian sol - diers, March - ing as to

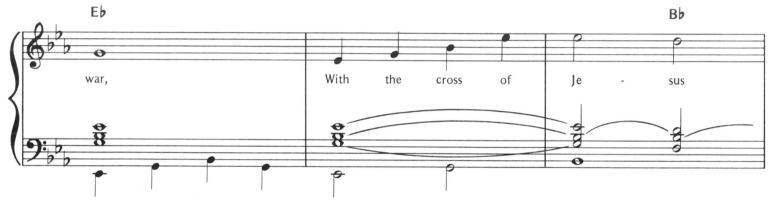

war, With the cross of Je - sus

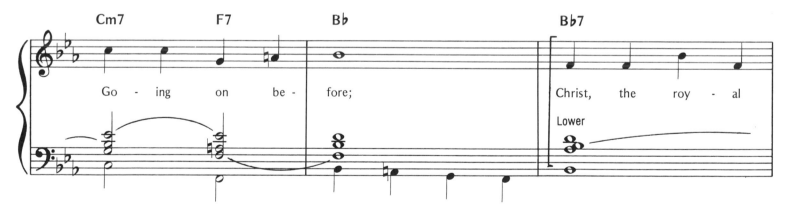

Go - ing on be - fore; Christ, the roy - al
Lower

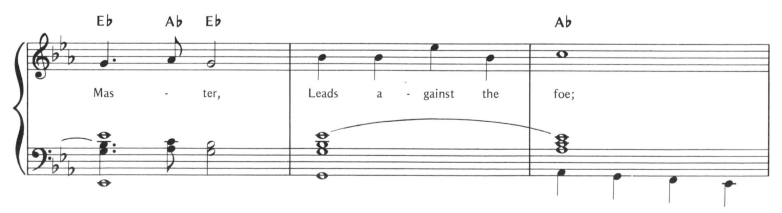

Mas - ter, Leads a - gainst the foe;

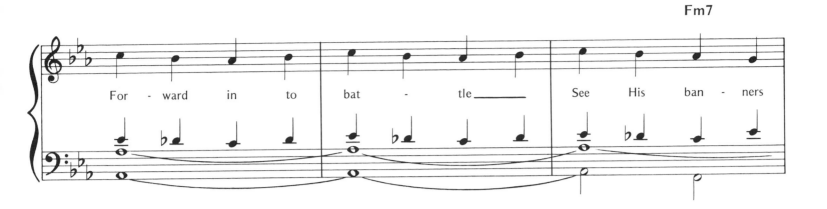

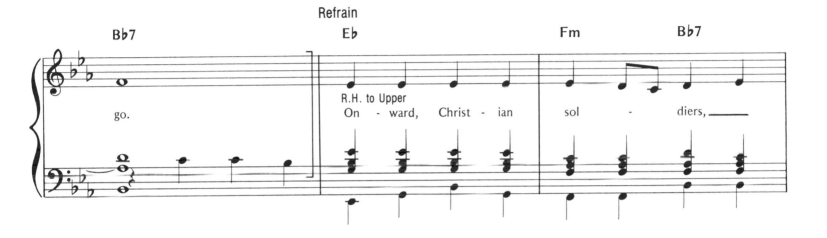

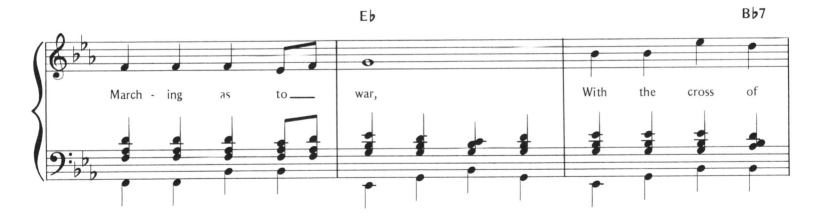

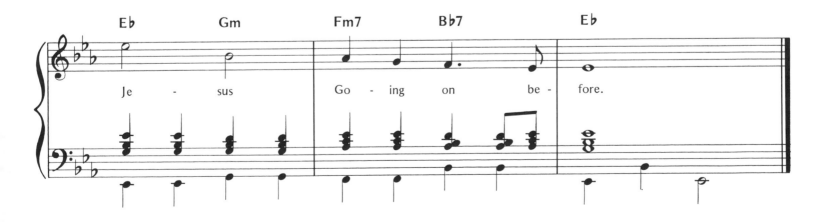

What A Friend We Have In Jesus

Registration 4

Words by Joseph Scriven
Music by Charles C. Converse

Holy! Holy! Holy!

Registration 11

Words by Reginald Heber
Music by John B. Dykes

Moderately slow

Ave Maria

Registration 14

Franz Schubert
Op. 52, No. 6

Slowly

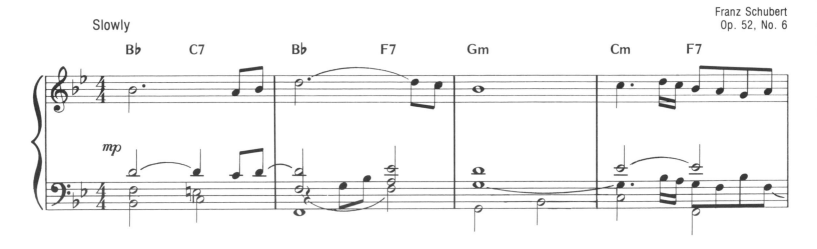

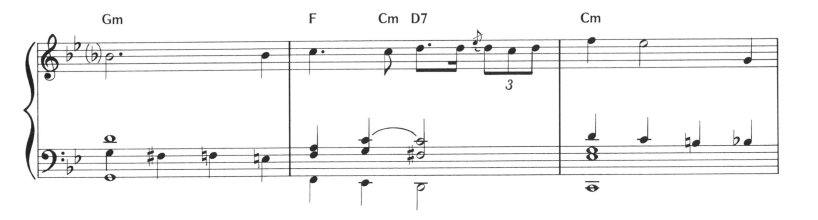

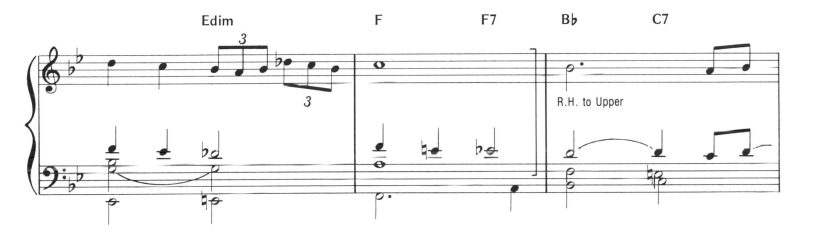

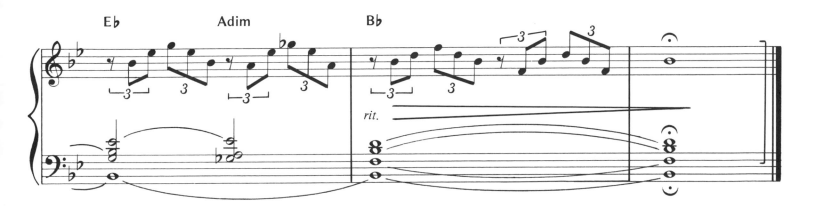

Nearer, My God, To Thee

Registration 18

Words by Sarah F. Adams
Music by Lowell Mason

Moderately slow

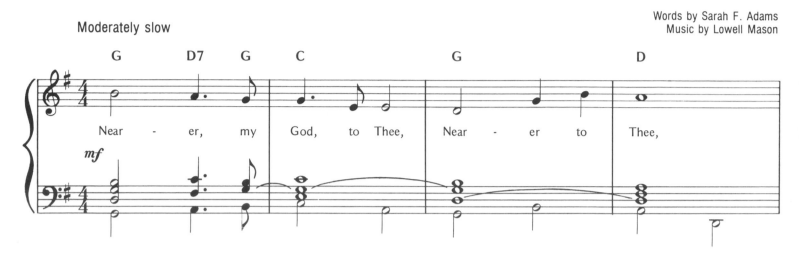

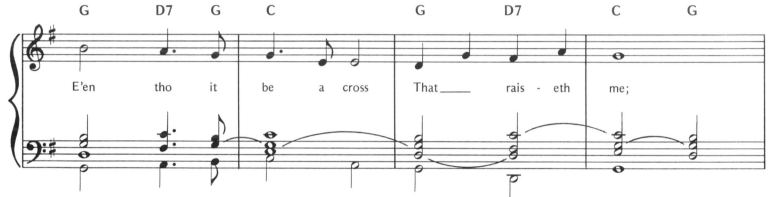

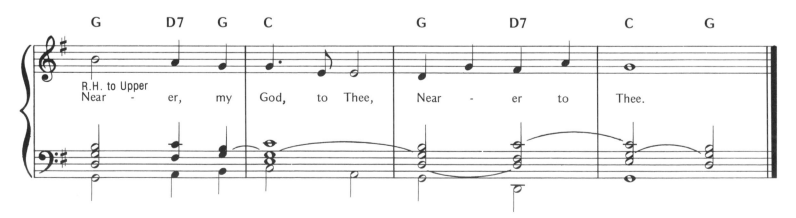

Jesus Loves Me

Registration 8

Words by Anna B. Warner
Music by William B. Bradbury

Moderately

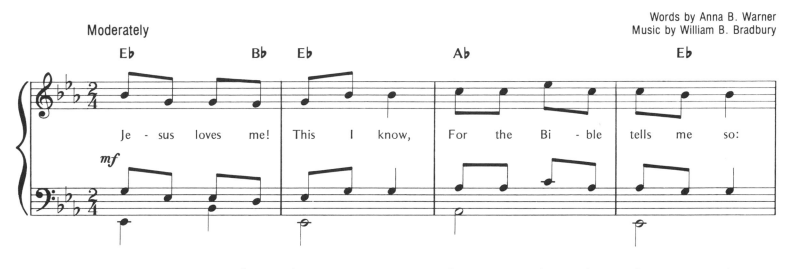

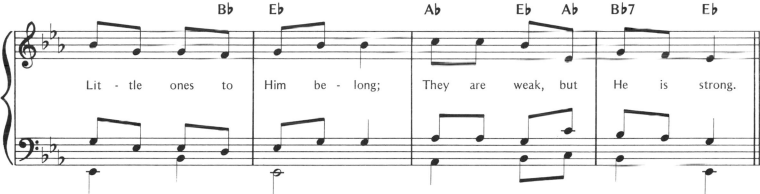

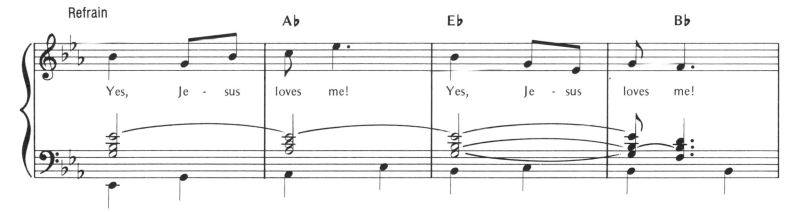

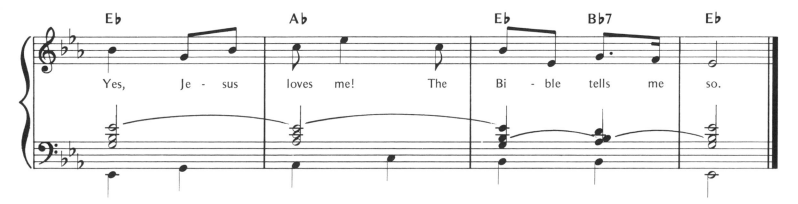

Pass Me Not, O Gentle Saviour

Registration 8

Words by Fanny J. Crosby
Music by William H. Doane

Moderately

Pass me not, O gen - tle Sav - ior, Hear my hum - ble cry,

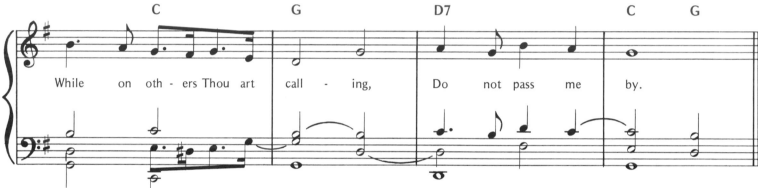

While on oth - ers Thou art call - ing, Do not pass me by.

Refrain

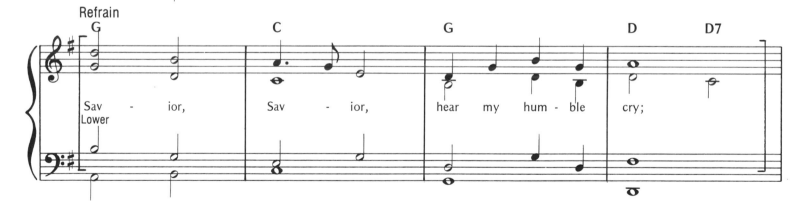

Sav - ior, Sav - ior, hear my hum - ble cry;
Lower

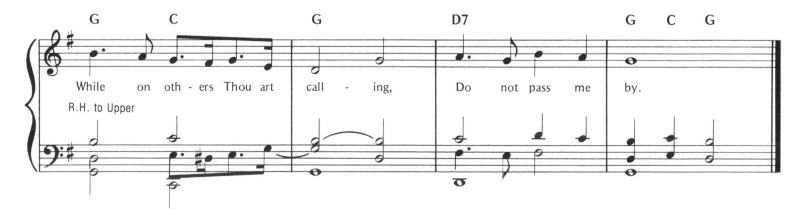

While on oth - ers Thou art call - ing, Do not pass me by.
R.H. to Upper

Rock Of Ages, Cleft For Me

Registration 5

Words by Augustus M. Toplady
Music by Thomas Hastings

Jesus, Lover Of My Soul

Registration 5

Words by Charles Wesley
Music by Simeon B. Marsh

Moderately

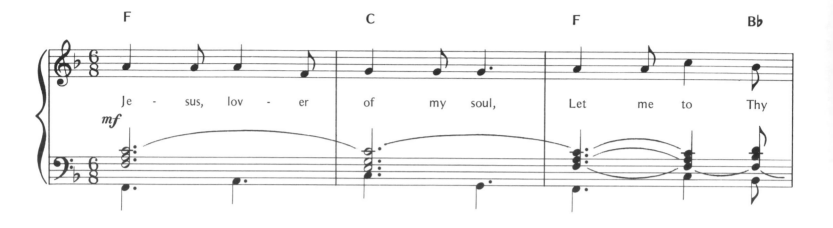

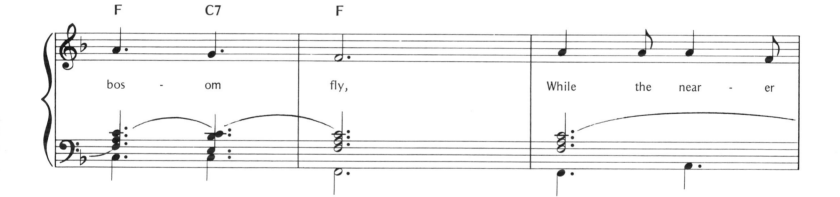

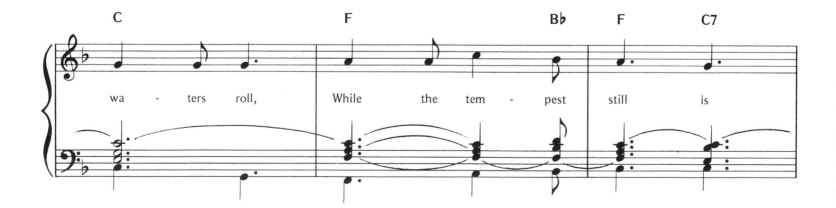

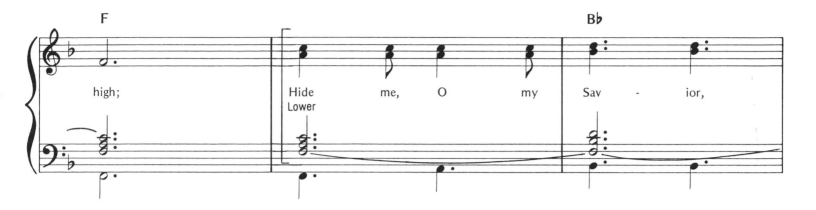

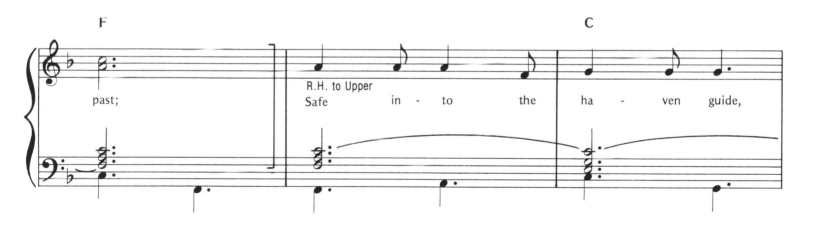

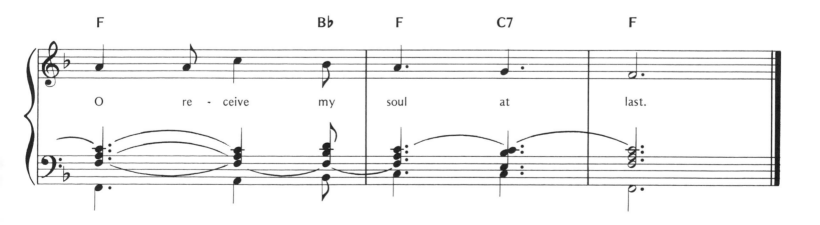

Bringing In The Sheaves

Registration 2

Words by Knowles Shaw
Music by Georges A. Minor

Abide With Me

Registration 7

Words by Henry Francis Lyte
Music by William H. Monk

Moderately slow

I Love Thy Kingdom, Lord

Registration 17

Words by Timothy Dwight
Music by Aaron Williams

Moderately slow

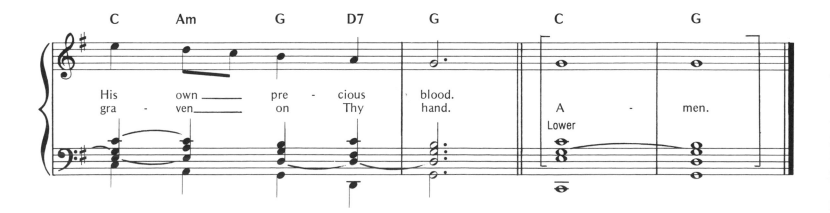

How Sweet The Name Of Jesus Sounds

Registration 20

Words by John Newton
Music by Alexander R. Rainagle

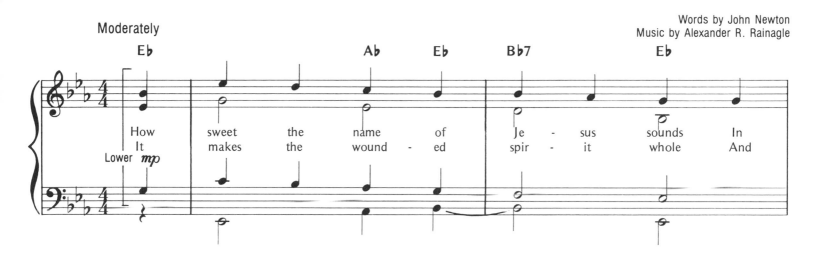

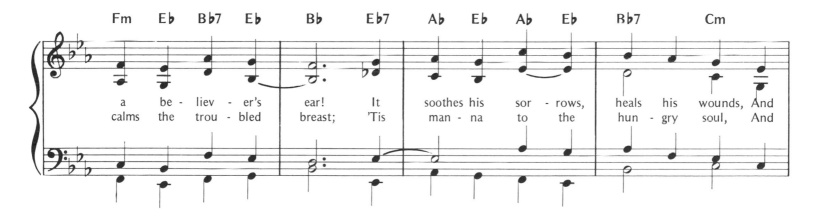

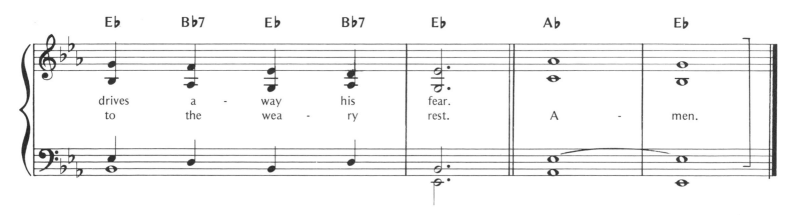

Faith Of Our Fathers

Registration 8

Words by Frederick W. Faber
Music by Henri F. Hemy

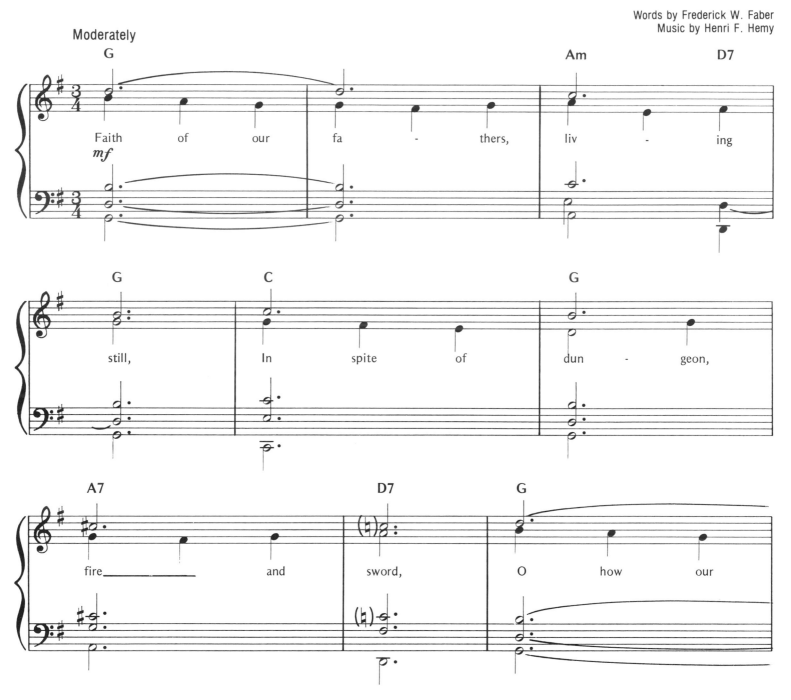

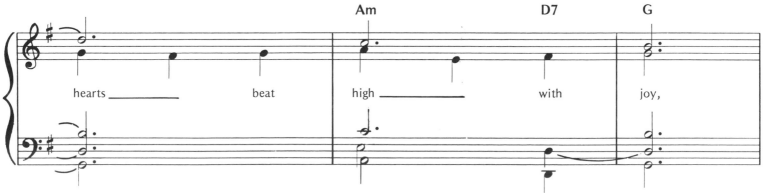

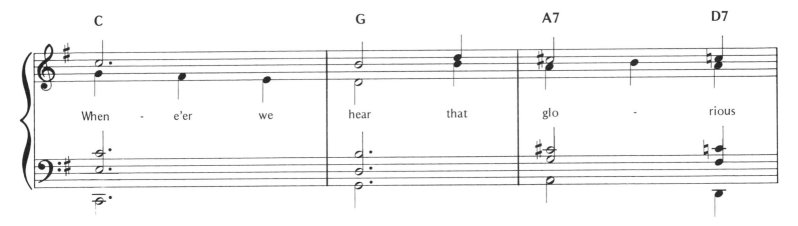

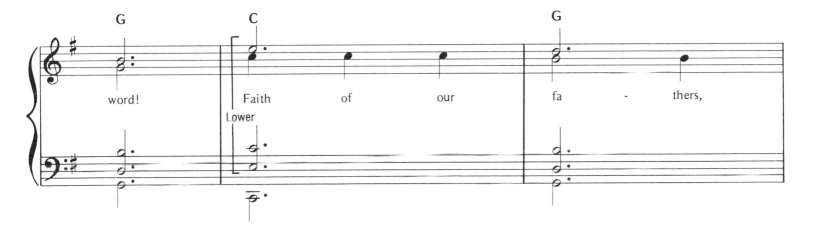

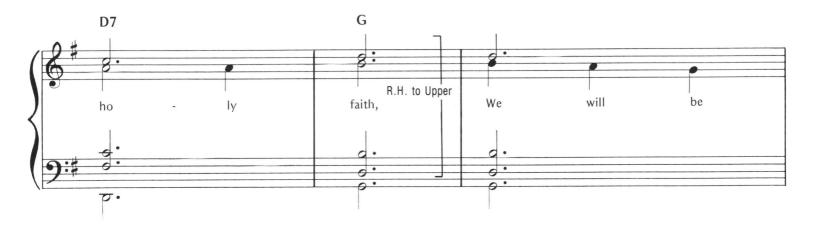

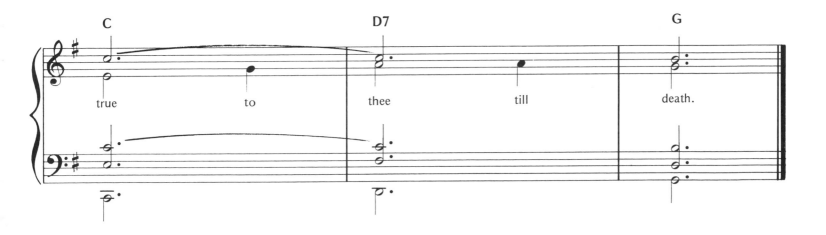

Blessed Assurance

Registration 16

Words by Fanny J. Crosby
Music by Phoebe P. Knapp

Amazing Grace

Registration 13

Words by John Newton
Early American Melody

Moderately slow

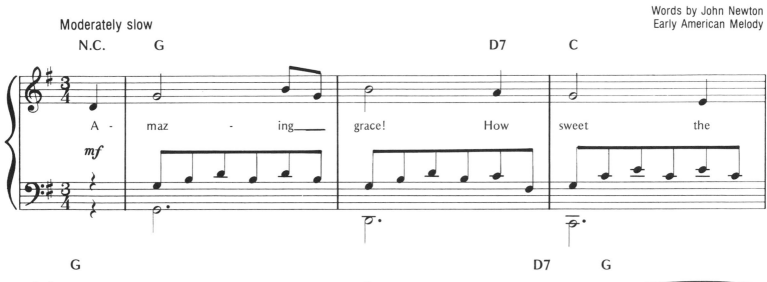

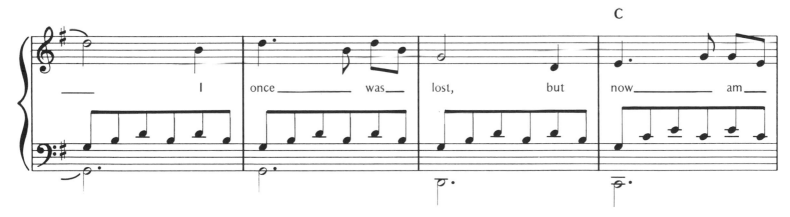

Beautiful Isle Of Somewhere

Registration 5

Moderately

Words by Jessie B. Pounds
Music by J.S. Fearis

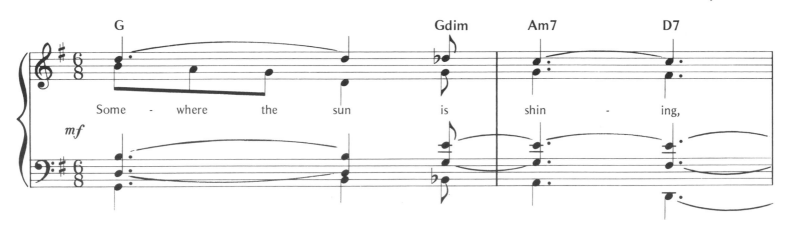

Some - where the sun is shin - ing,

Some - where the song - birds dwell; _____

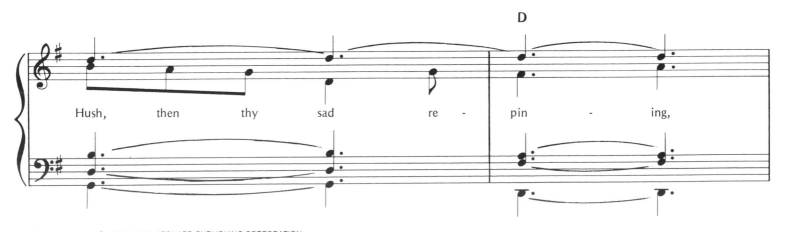

Hush, then thy sad re - pin - ing,

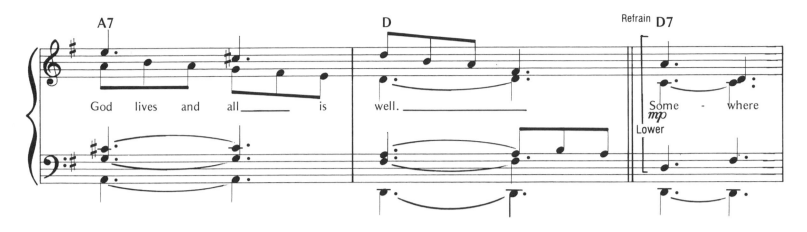
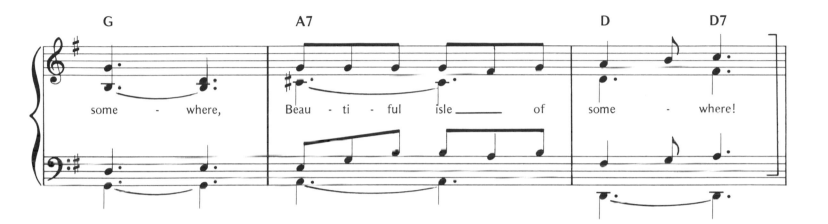
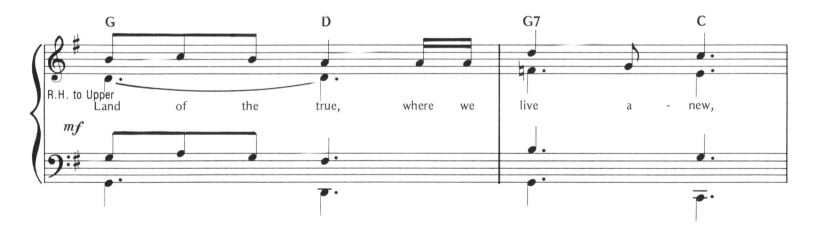
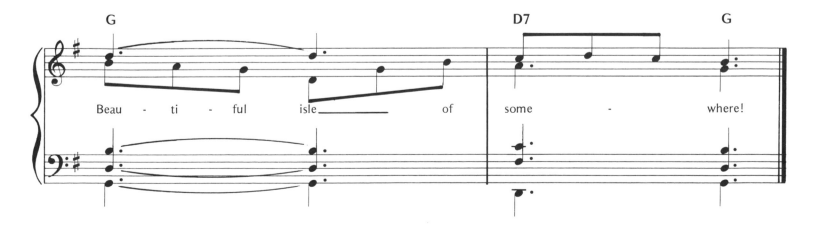

27

This Is My Father's World

Registration 15

Words by Maltbie D. Babcock
Traditional English Melody

Moderately slow

This is my Fa-ther's world, And to my lis-t'ning ears All

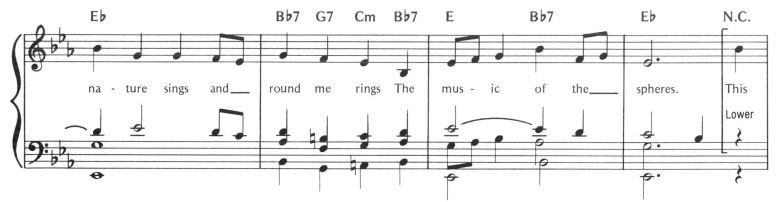

na-ture sings and round me rings The mus-ic of the spheres. This

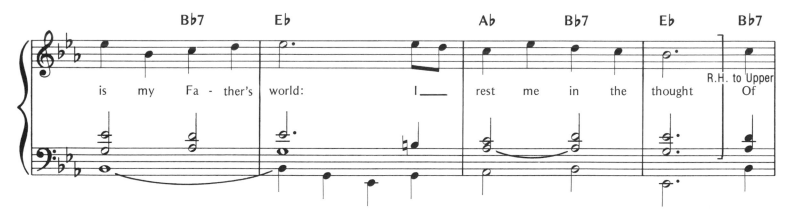

is my Fa-ther's world: I rest me in the thought Of

rocks and trees, of skies and seas; His hand the won-ders wrought.

Praise To The Lord, The Almighty

Registration 5

Words by Catherine Winkworth
Music from ''Praxis Pietatis Melica''

O Perfect Love

Registration 15

Words by Dorothy B. Gurney
Music by Joseph Barnby

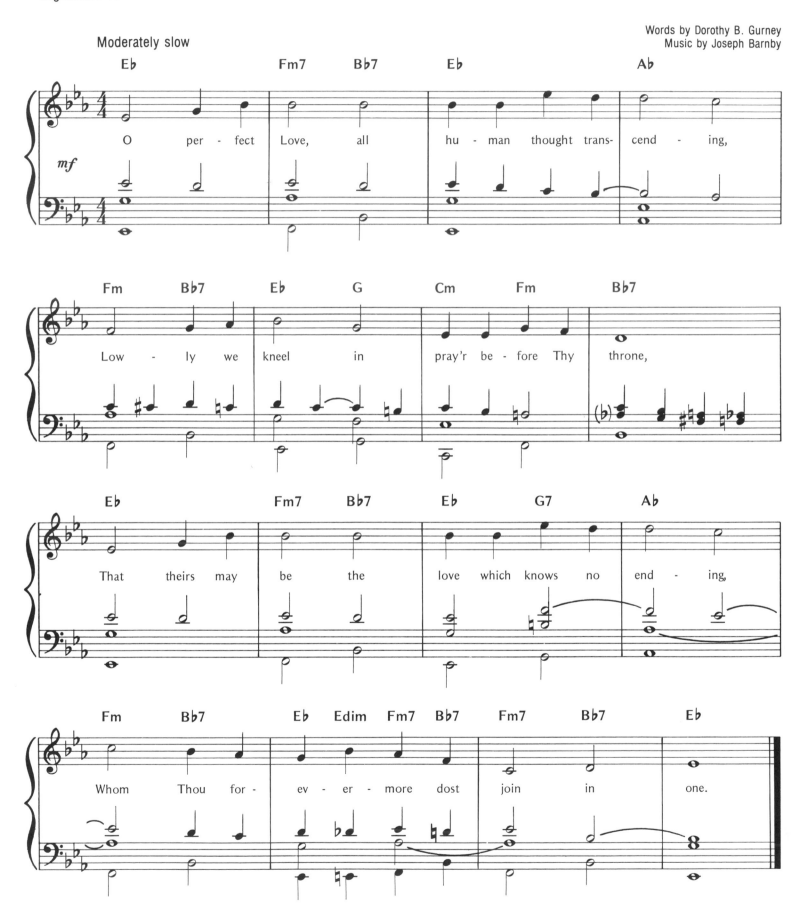

I Surrender All

Registration 18

Words by Judson W. Van DeVenter
Music by Winfield S. Weeden

Be Still, My Soul

Registration 4

Words by Katharina von Schlegel
Music by Jan Sibelius

Moderately slow

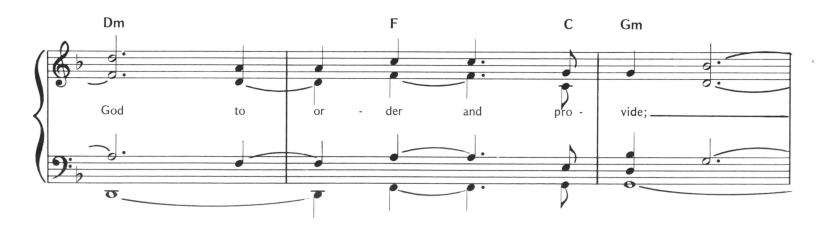

33

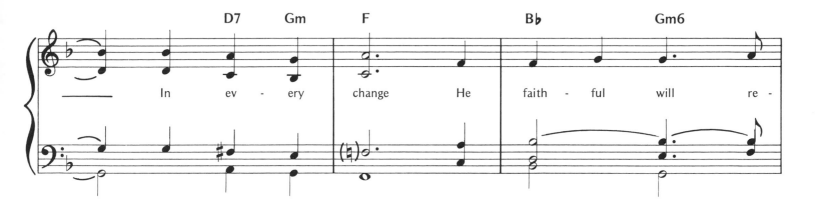

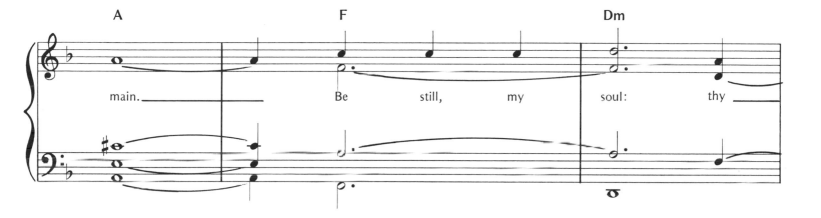

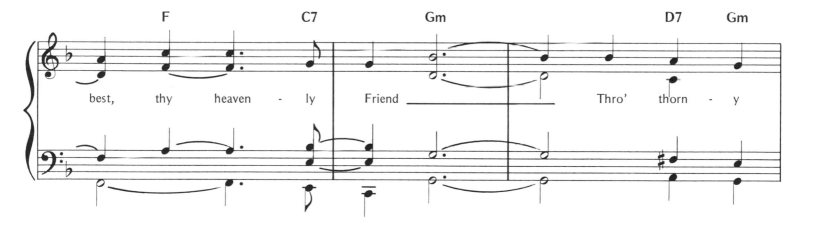

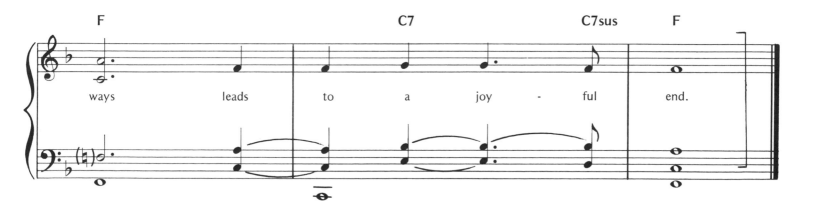

Are You Washed In The Blood?

Registration 7

Words and Music by
E.A. Hoffman

My Faith Looks Up To Thee

Registration 11

Words by Ray Palmer
Music by Lowell Mason

Moderately slow

Kum Ba Ya

Registration 1

Slowly

Nigerian Folk Song

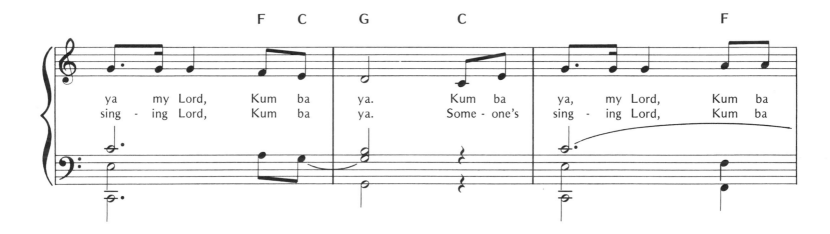

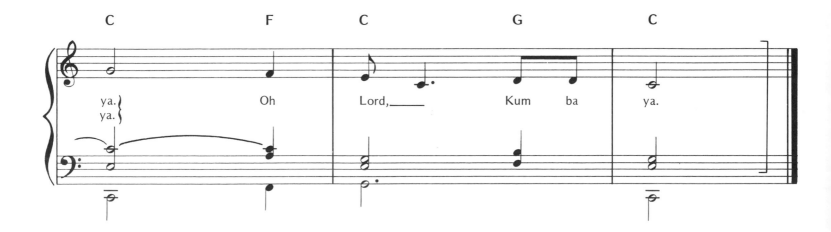

The Lord's My Shepherd

Registration 14

Words from Psalm 23
Music by William H. Havergal

Moderately slow

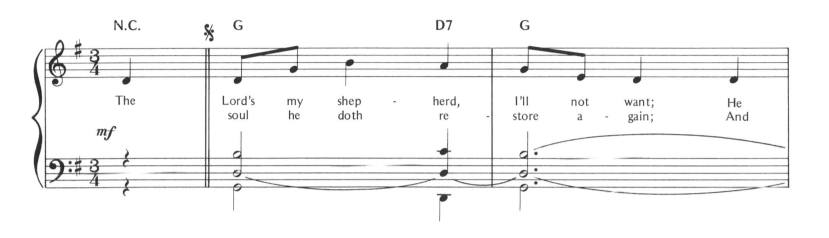

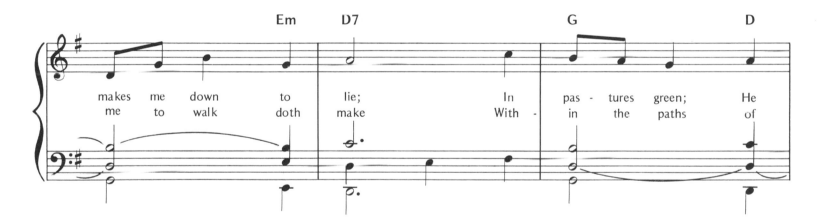

O Worship The King, All Glorious Above

Registration 19

Words by Robert Grant
Music by Johann Michael Haydn

Moderately

O wor - ship the King all glo - rious a-

bove, O grate - ful - ly sing His pow'r___ and His

Love; Our Shield and De - fend - er, the An - cient of

days, Pa - vil - ioned in splen - dor, and gird - ed with praise.

Shall We Meet Beyond The River

Registration 17

Words by H.L. Hastings
Music by Elihu S. Rice

The Rosary

Registration 17

Slowly

Words — Anonymous
Music by Ethelbert Nevin

Vib./Trem.: Off

The hours I spend with thee, dear heart,
Each hour a pearl, with each pearl a pray'r,

Are as a string of pearls to me;
To still a heart in ab - sence wrung.

I count them o - ver ev - 'ry
I tell each bead un - to the

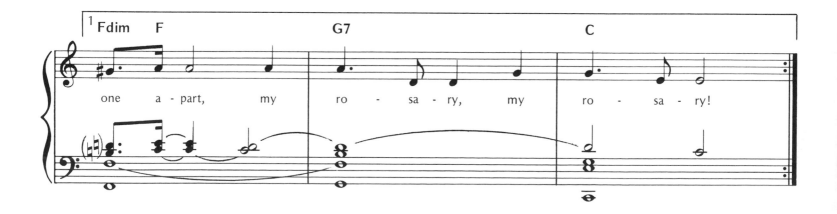

one a - part, my ro - sa - ry, my ro - sa - ry!

41

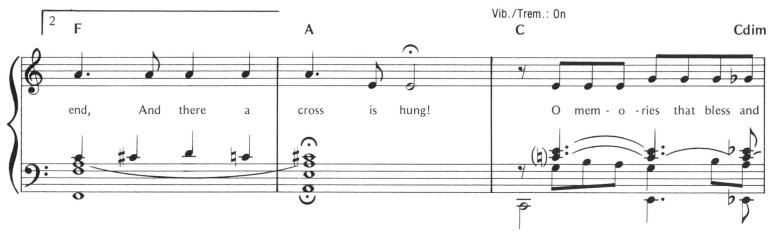

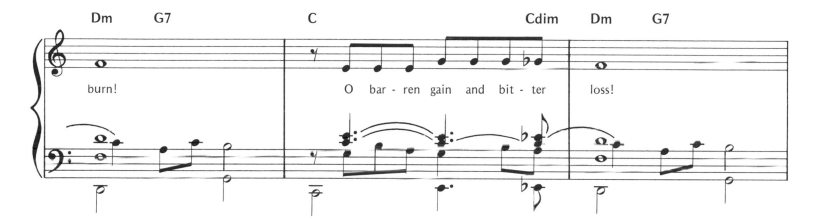

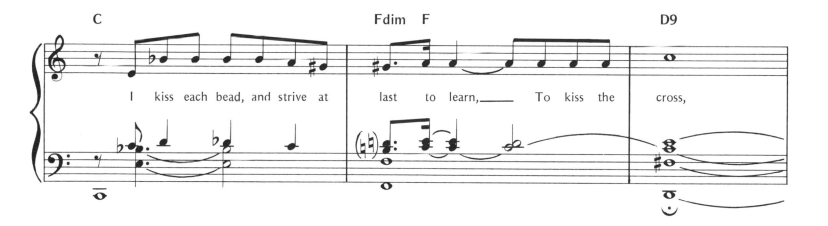

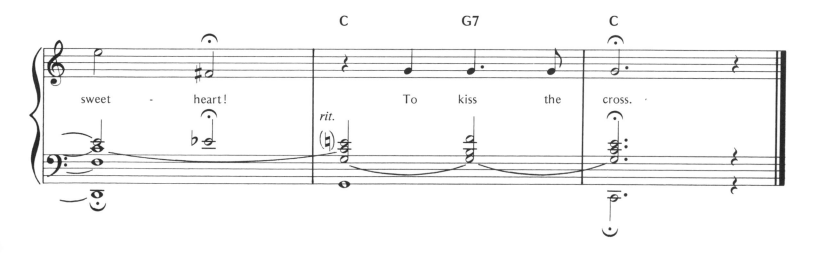

Leaning On The Everlasting Arms

Registration 8

Words by Elisha A. Hoffman
Music by Anthony J. Showalter

Jesus Saves

Registration 2

Words by Priscilla J. Owens
Music by William J. Kirkpatrick

Moderately

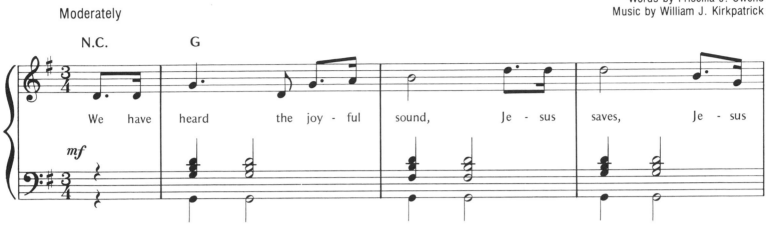

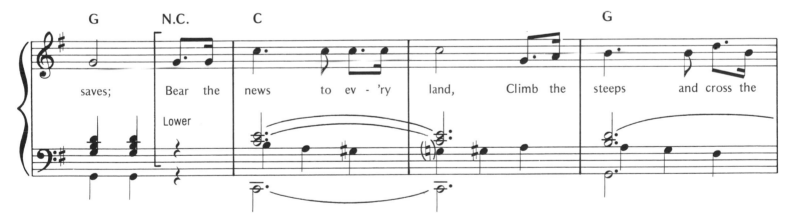

O Sacred Head, Now Wounded

Registration 19

Words by Bernard of Clairvaux
Music by Hans Leo Hassler

All Glory, Laud And Honor

Registration 6

Words by St. Theodulph of Orleans
Music by Melchior Teschner

Blest Be The Tie That Binds

Registration 9

Words by John Fawcett
Music by Hans G. Nageli

Moderately

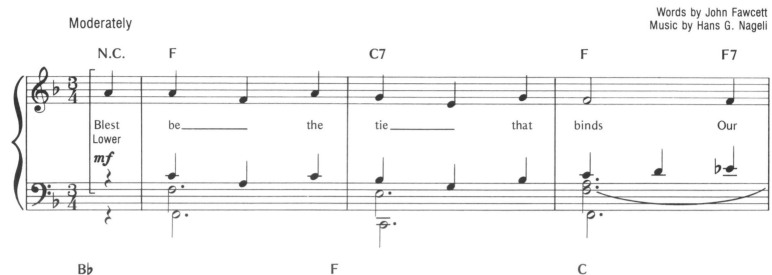

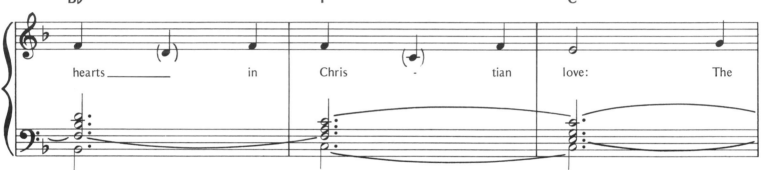

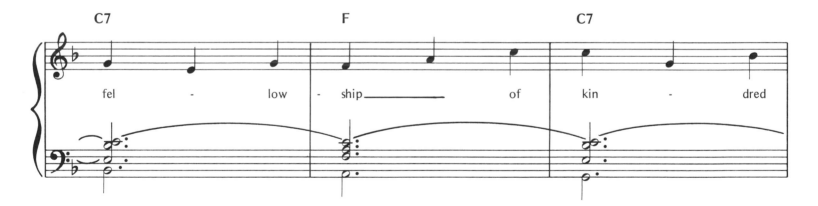

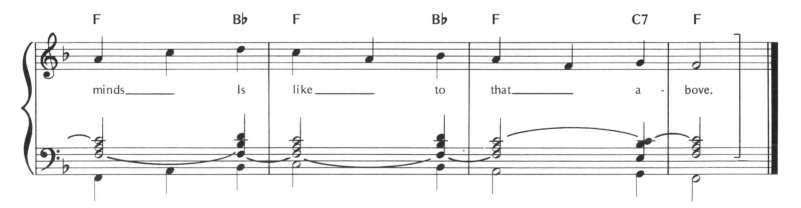

I Know That My Redeemer Lives

Registration 12

Words by Samuel Medley
Music by John Hatton

The Holy City

Registration 16

Words by Fred Weatherly
Music by Stephen Adams

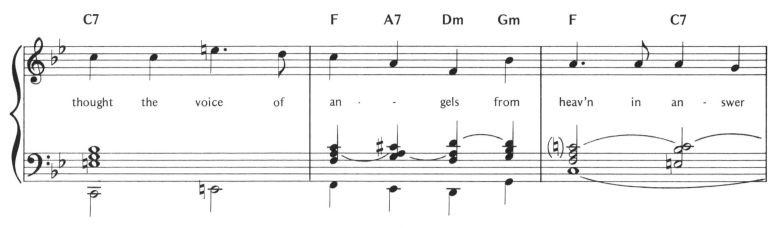

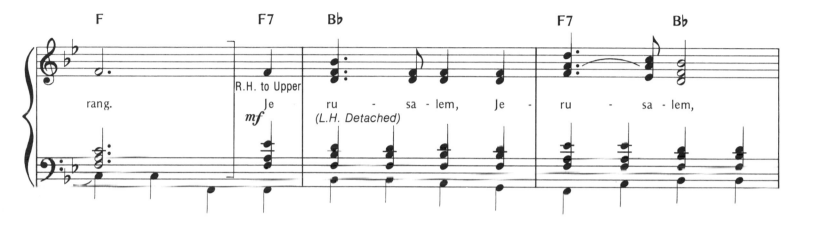

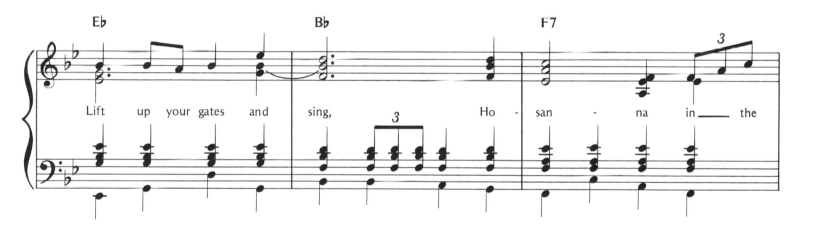

Were You There?

Registration 17

Slowly

Negro Spiritual

Saviour, Like A Shepherd Lead Us

Registration 8

Words by Dorothy A. Thrupp
Music by William B. Bradbury

Moderately slow

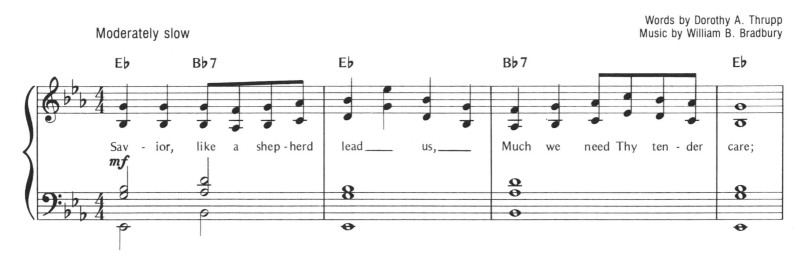

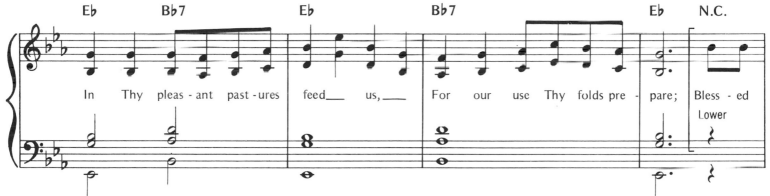

Stand Up! Stand Up For Jesus

Registration 10

Words by George Duffield
Music by George J. Webb

Still, Still With Thee

Registration 14

Words by Harriet B. Stowe
Music by Felix Mendelssohn-Bartholdy

When The Roll Is Called Up Yonder

Registration 2

Moderately with spirit

Words and Music by
James M. Black

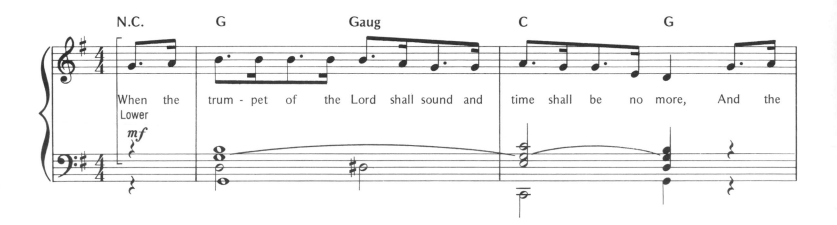

When the trum - pet of the Lord shall sound and time shall be no more, And the

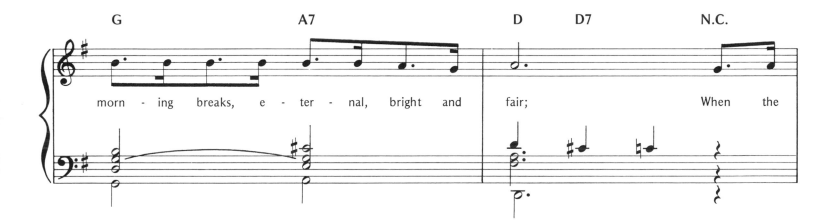

morn - ing breaks, e - ter - nal, bright and fair; When the

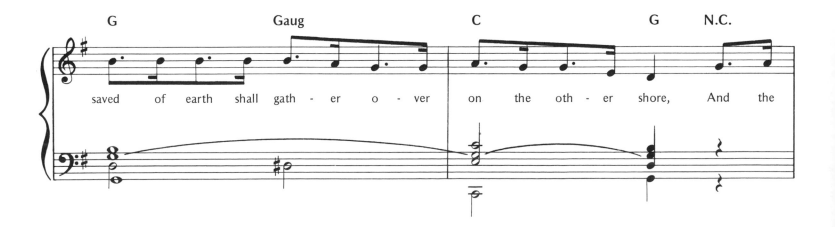

saved of earth shall gath - er o - ver on the oth - er shore, And the

Come, Thou Almighty King

Registration 15

Moderately

Words — Anonymous
Music by Felice di Giardini

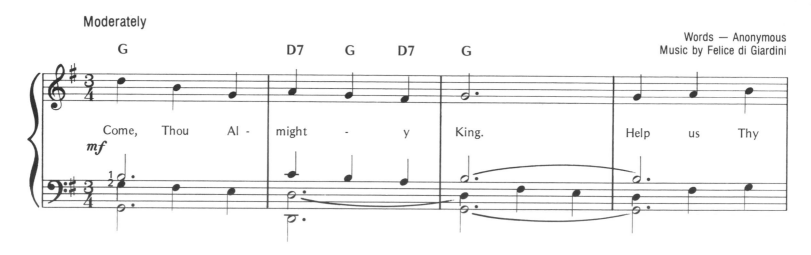

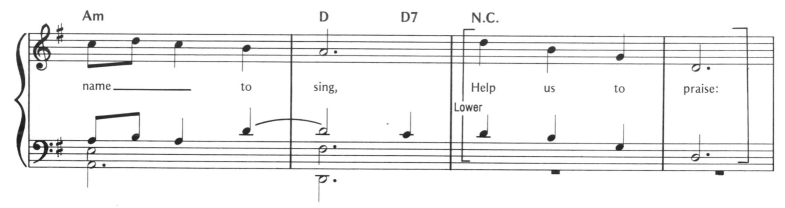

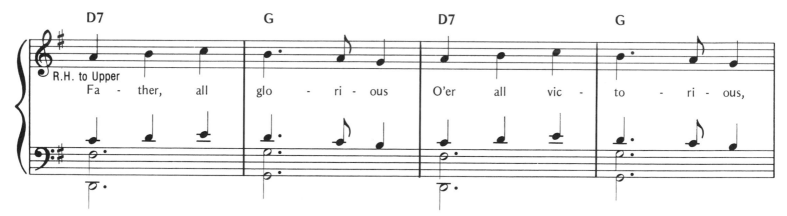

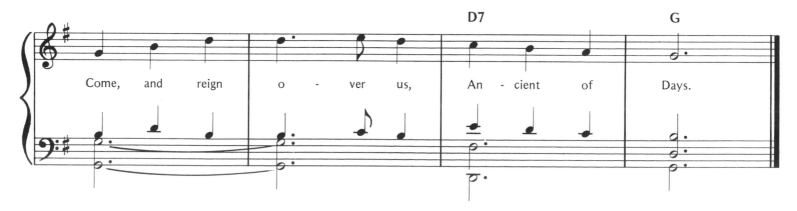

All Hail The Power Of Jesus' Name!

Registration 5

Words by Edward Perronet
Music by Oliver Holden

Majestically

Christ The Lord Is Risen Today

Registration 11

Words by Charles Wesley
Music from ''Lyra Davidica''

Down By The Riverside

Registration 8

Words — Anonymous
Negro Spiritual

Moderately slow

The Church's One Foundation

Registration 2

Words by Samuel J. Stone
Music by Samuel S. Wesley

Open Now Thy Gates Of Beauty

Registration 3

Words by Catherine Winkworth
Music by Joachim Neander

Moderately slow

A Parting Hymn We Sing

Registration 20

Words by Aaron R. Wolfe
Music by Lowell Mason

Moderately

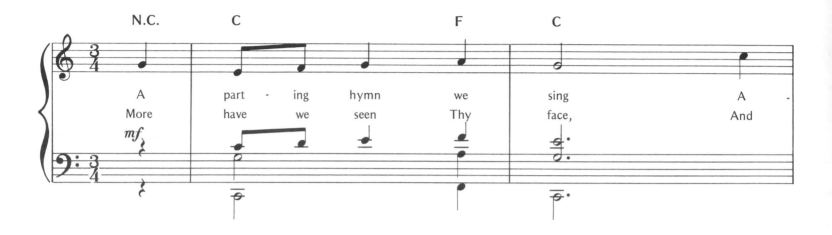

Awake, My Soul, And With The Sun

Registration 20

Made in U.S.A.

Words by Samuel Medley
Western Melody

Moderately

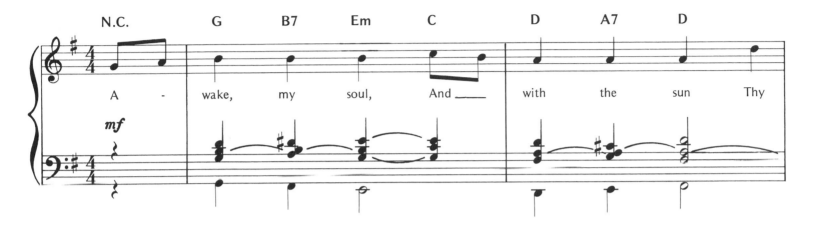

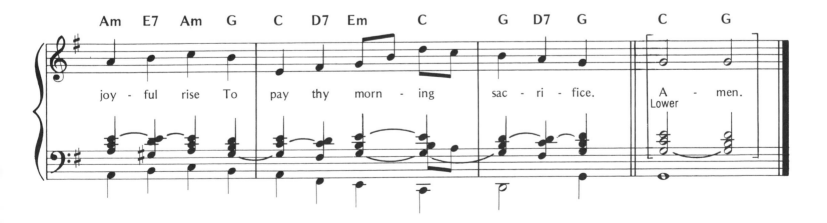

Cleanse Me

Registration 11

Words by Edwin Orr
Maori Melody

Slowly

Search me, O God, _____ and

know my heart to - day; _____

Try me, O Sav - ior,

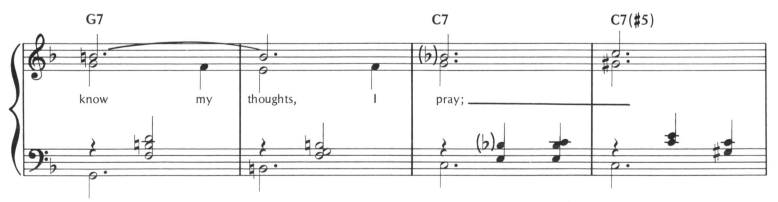

know my thoughts, I pray; _____

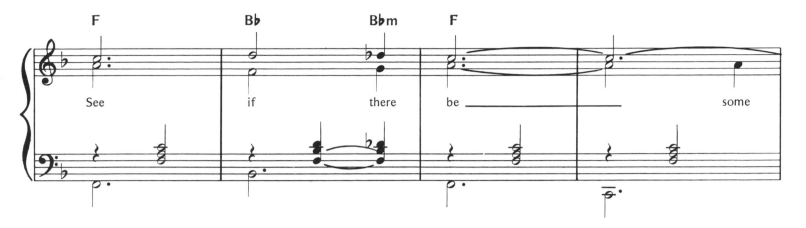

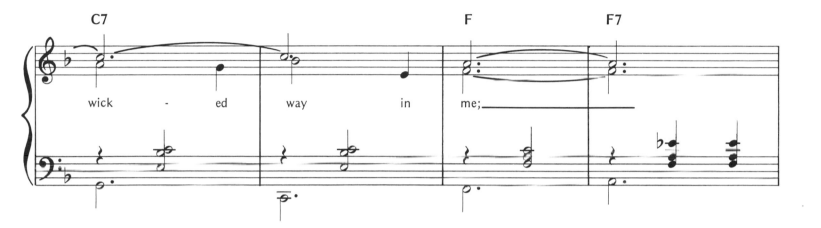

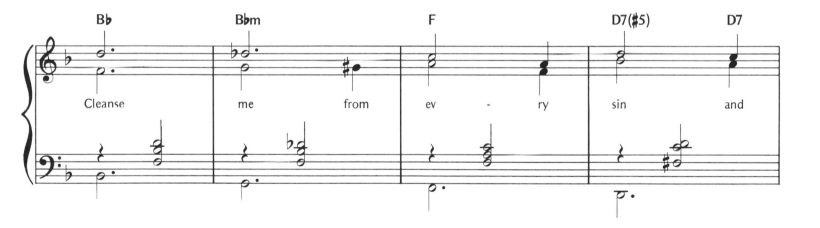

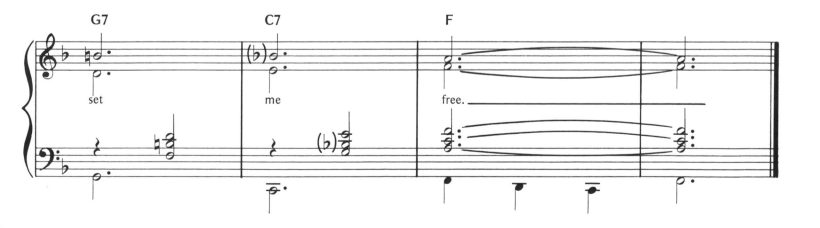

Our God, Our Help In Ages Past

Registration 1

Words by Isaac Watts
Music by William Croft

Moderately slow

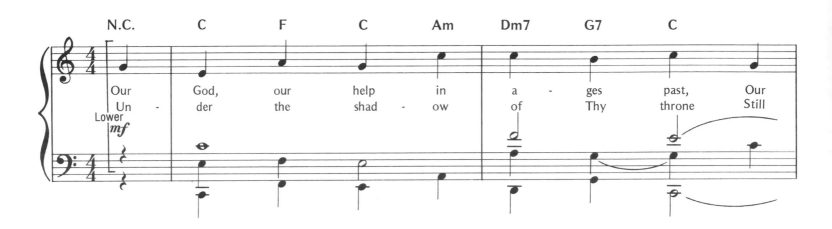

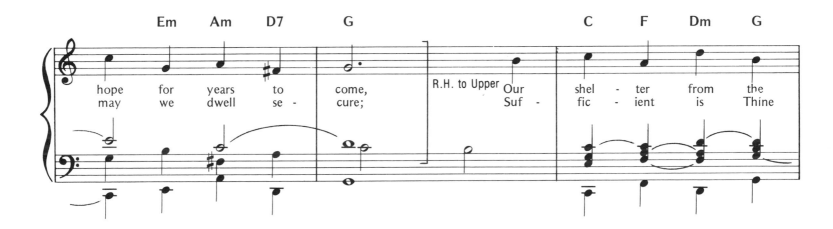

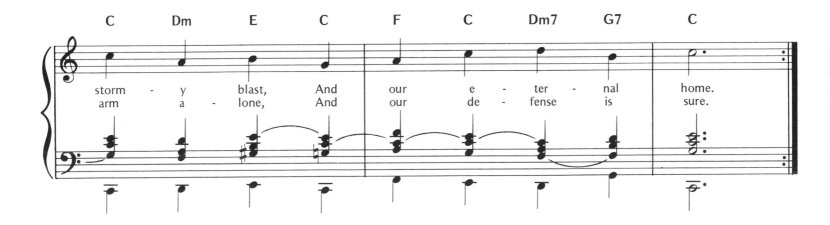

Jesus, Savior, Pilot Me

Registration 17

Words by Edward Hopper
Music by John E. Gould

When I Survey The Wondrous Cross

Registration 6

Words by Isaac Watts
Music by Lowell Mason

These Things Shall Be: A Loftier Race

Registration 11

Words by John A. Symonds
Ancient Hymn Tune

Hosanna, Loud Hosanna

Registration 2

Words by Jeanette Threlfall
Music from a German ''Gesangbuch''

Majestically

Vib./Trem.: Off
Unison

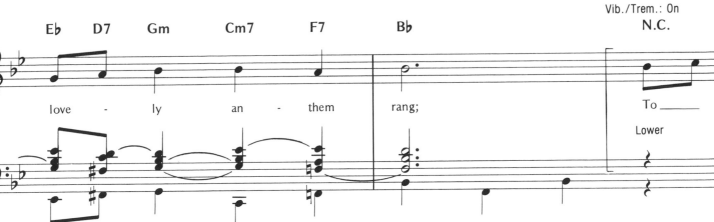

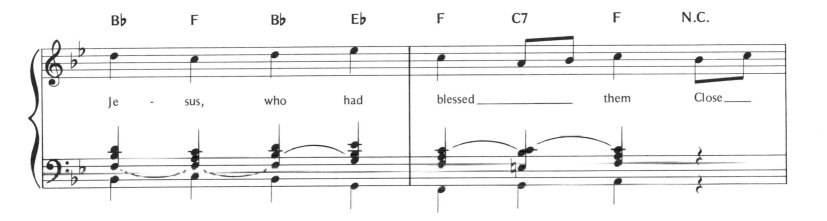

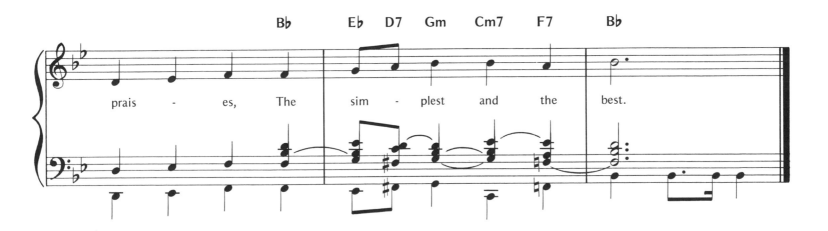

Come, Christians, Join To Sing

Registration 5

Words by Christian H. Bateman
Music Anonymous

Before The Lord, We Bow

Registration 13

Words by Francis S. Key
Music by John Darwall

Moderately slow

Once To Ev'ry Man And Nation

Registration 12

Words by James R. Lowell
Welsh Hymn Melody

Jesus Shall Reign Where'er The Sun

Registration 14

Words by Isaac Watts
Music by John Hatton

All Things Bright And Beautiful

Registration 7

Words by Cecil F. Alexander
Music by William H. Monk

77

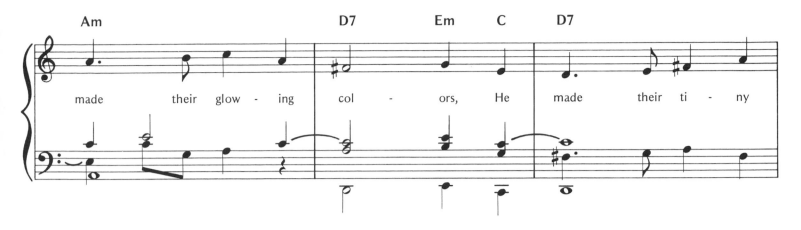

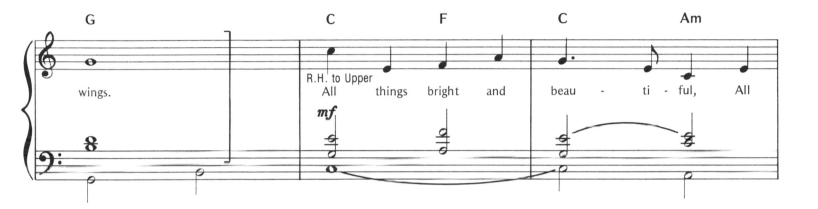

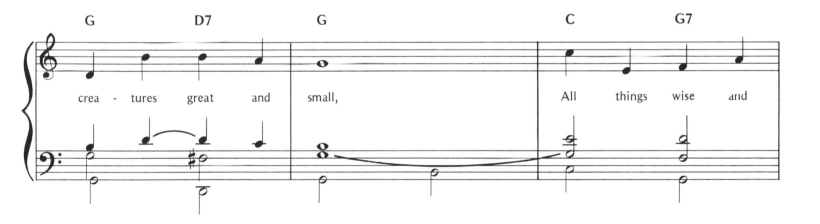

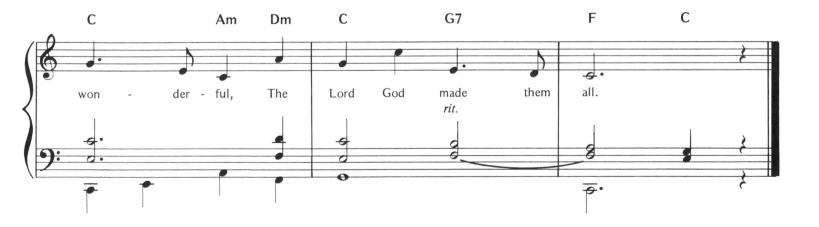

Saviour, Breathe An Evening Blessing

Registration 14

Words by James Edmeston
Music by George C. Stebbins

Moderately slow

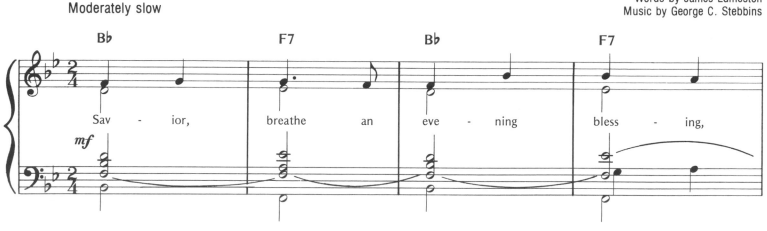

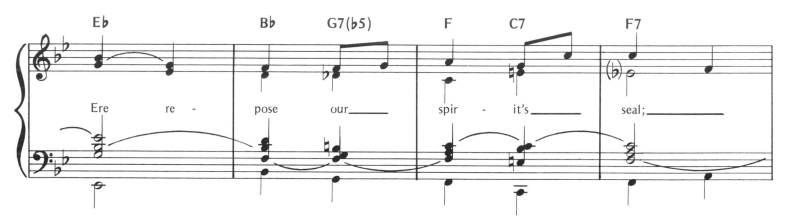

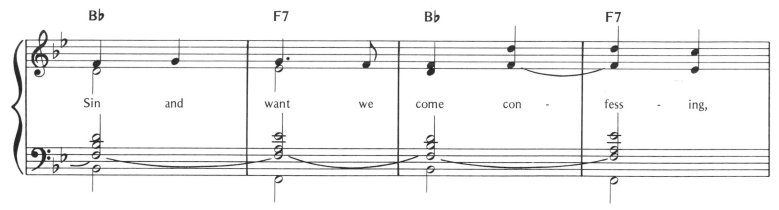

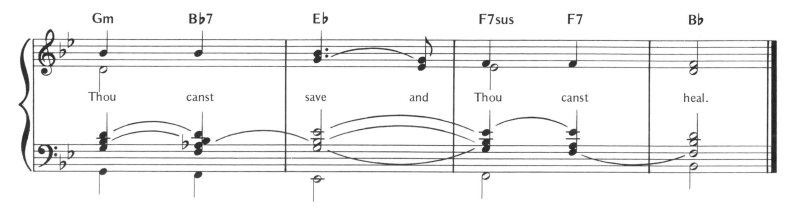

Now Thank We All Our God

Registration 2

Words by Martin Rinkart
Music by Johann Cruger

Jesus, Still Lead On

Registration 6

Moderately slow

Words by Nicolaus L. Zinzendorf
Music by Adam Drese

Standing On The Promises

Registration 3

Words and Music by
R. Kelso Carter

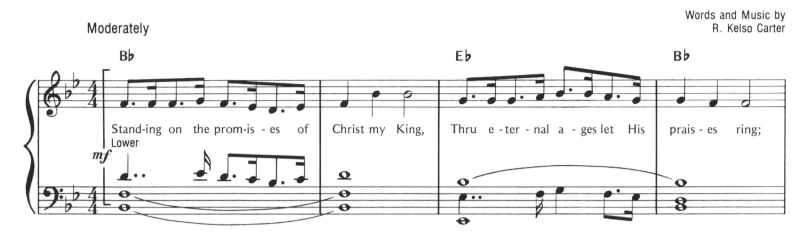

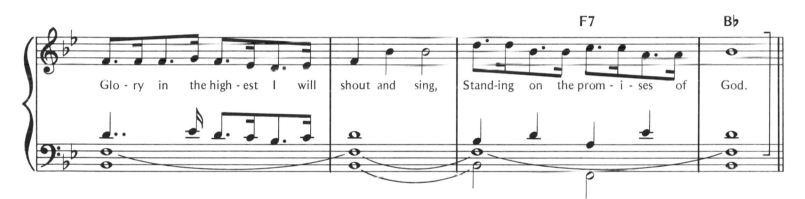

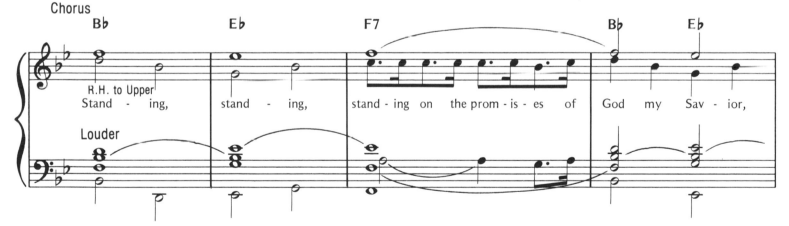

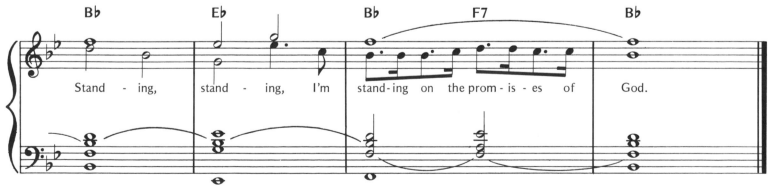

Swing Low, Sweet Chariot

Registration 19

Moderately slow

Spiritual

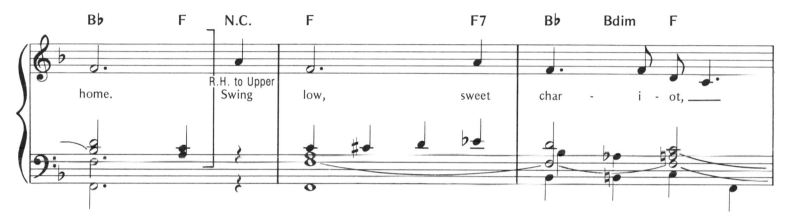

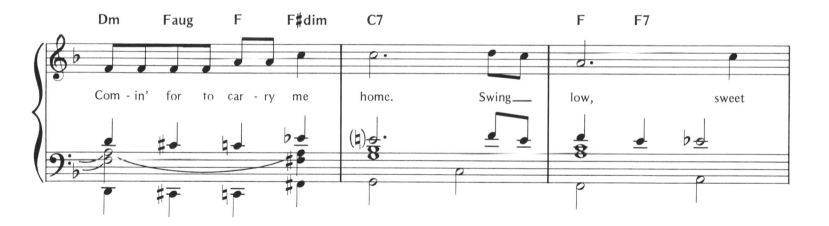

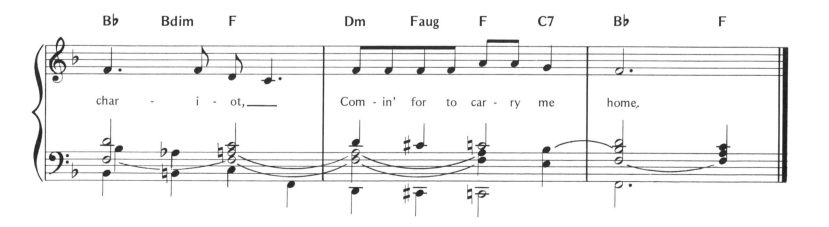

Am I A Soldier Of The Cross

Registration 3

Words by Isaac Watts
Music by Thomas A. Arne

Moderately

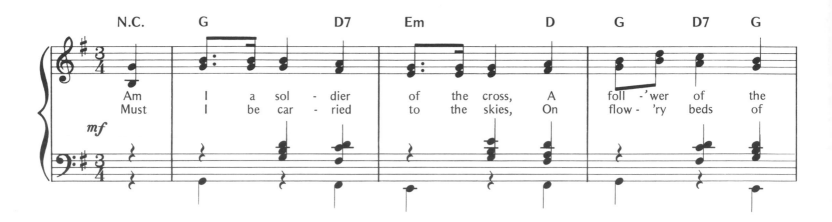

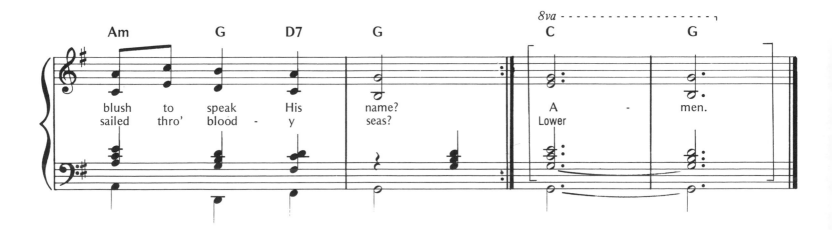

Now The Day Is Over

Registration 5

Moderately

Words by Sabine Baring-Gould
Music by Joseph Barnby

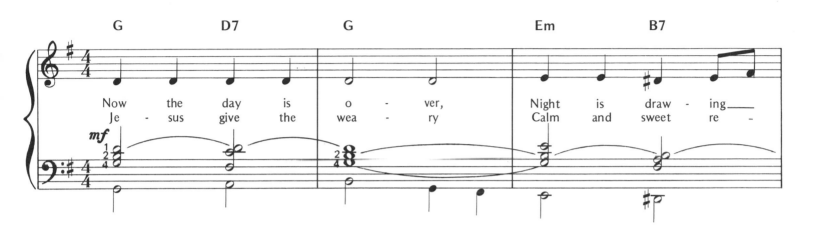

Now the day is o - ver,
Je - sus give the wea - ry
Night is draw - ing nigh,
Calm and sweet re - pose;

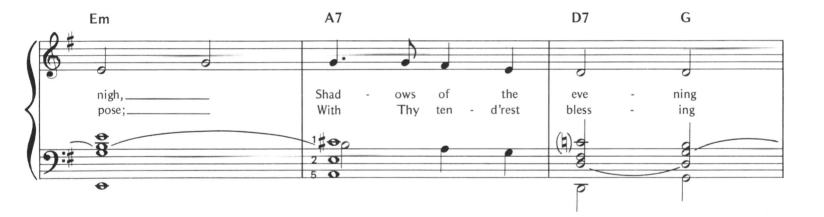

Shad - ows of the eve - ning
With Thy ten - d'rest bless - ing

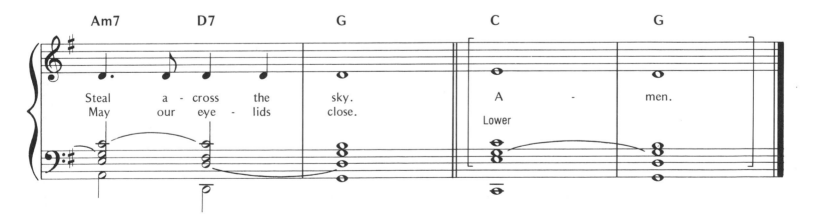

Steal a - cross the sky.
May our eye - lids close.
A - men.

Lower

Fairest Lord Jesus

Registration 18

Crusader's Hymn
Music by Richard S. Willis

Moderately

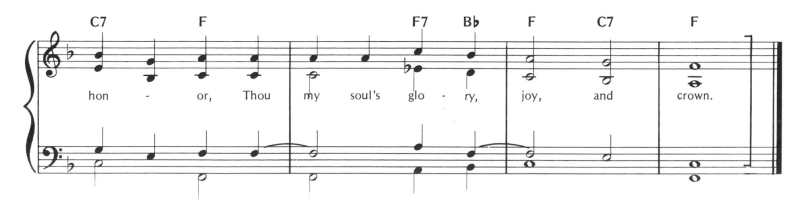

Shall We Gather At The River?

Registration 11

Words and Music by
Robert Lowry

The Wayfaring Stranger

Registration 20

Slowly

Spiritual

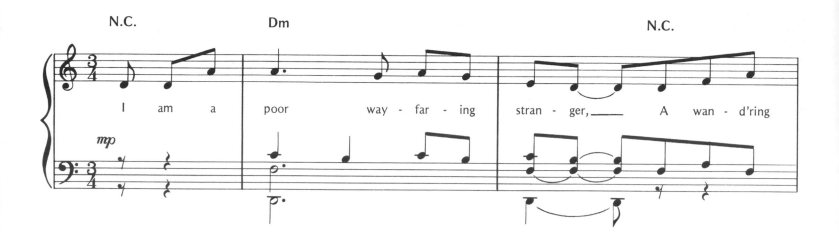

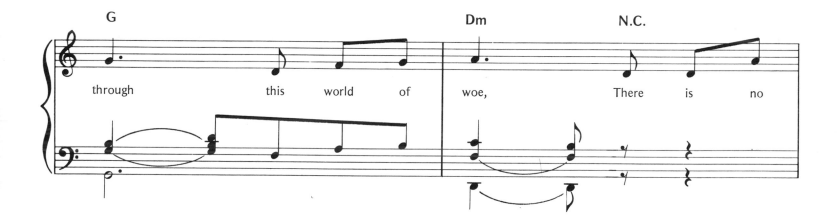

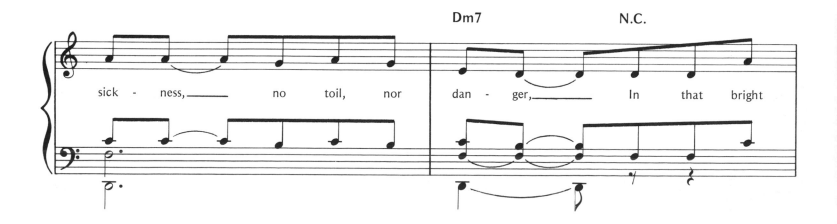

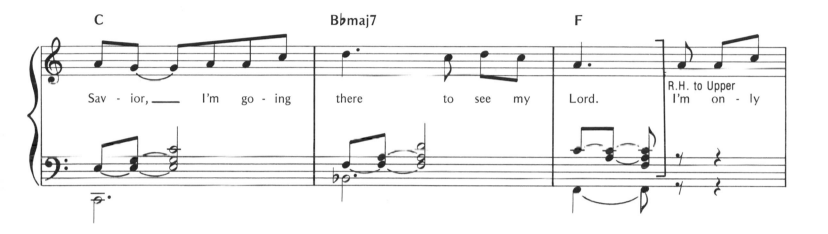

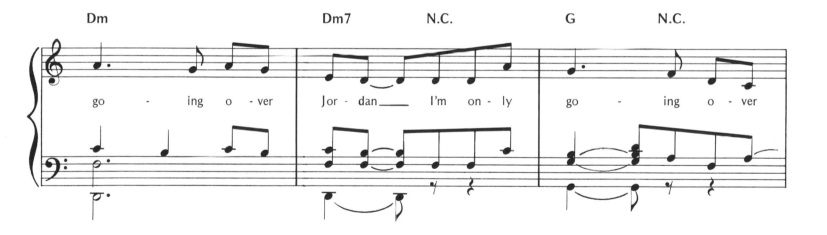

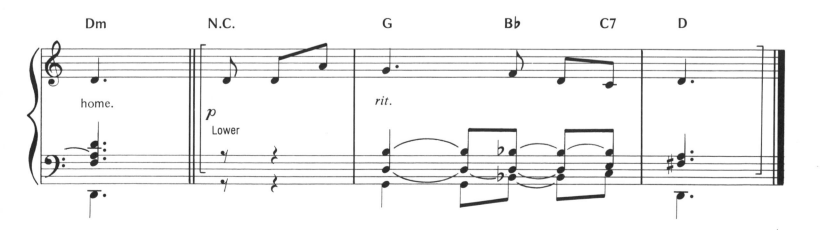

From Greenland's Icy Mountains

Registration 18

Words by Reginald Heber
Music by Lowell Mason

Saviour, When In Dust To Thee

Registration 3

Words by Robert Grant
Old Spanish Melody

I Love To Tell The Story

Registration 16

Words by Katherine Hankey
Music by William G. Fischer

Moderately

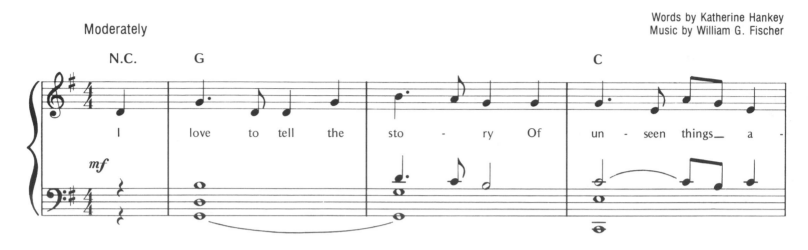

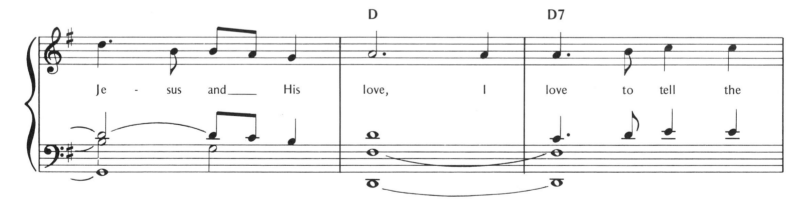

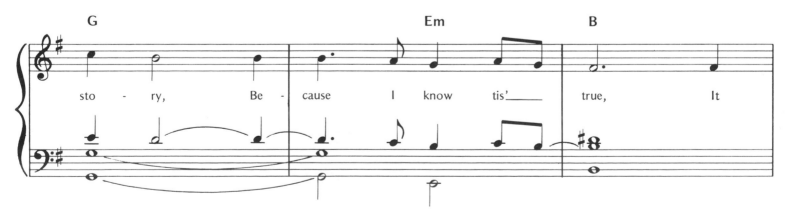

93

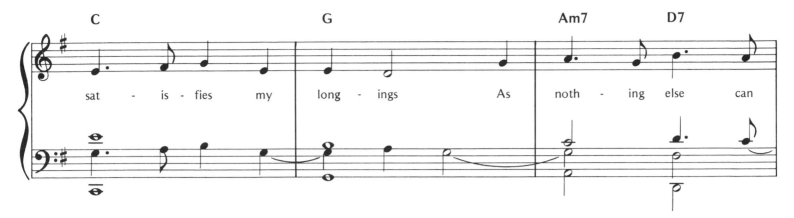

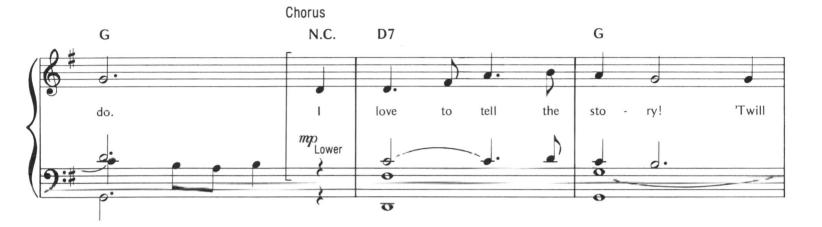

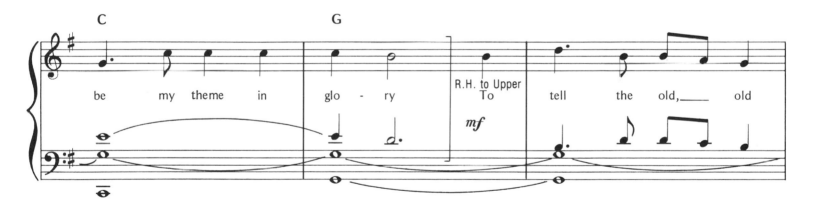

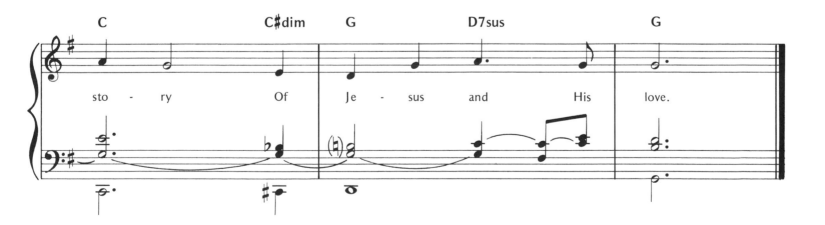

Jesus Christ Is Risen Today

Registration 3

Words by Charles Wesley
Music by Robert Williams

Moderately

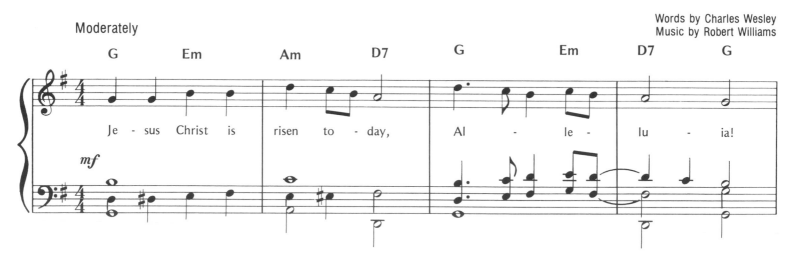

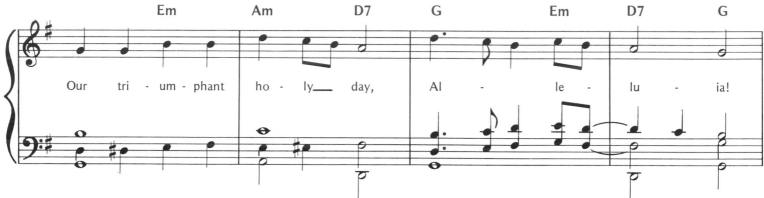

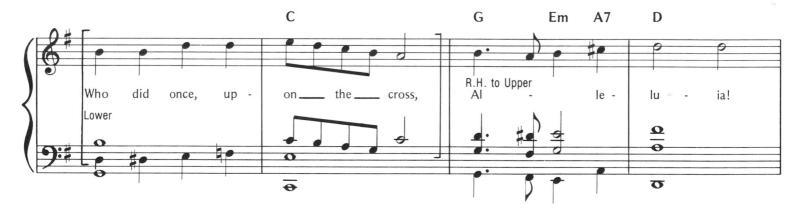

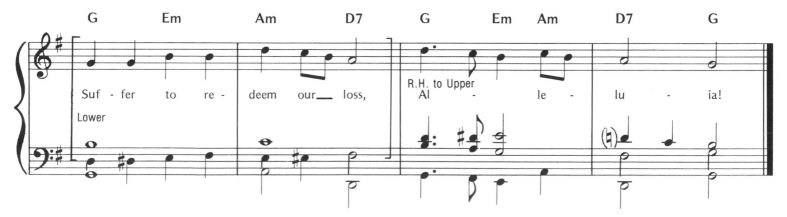

Praise Him, All Ye Little Children

Registration 10

Moderately slow

Anonymous

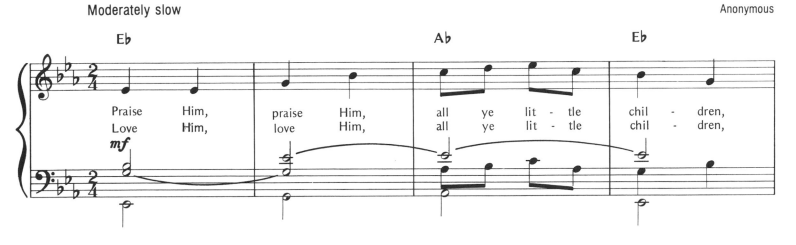

Praise Him, praise Him, all ye lit - tle chil - dren,
Love Him, love Him, all ye lit - tle chil - dren,

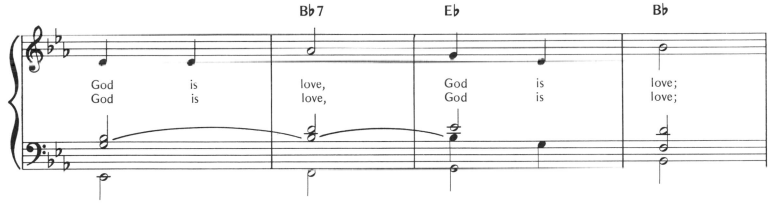

God is love, God is love;
God is love, God is love;

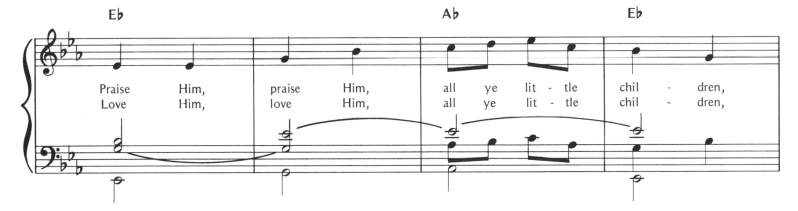

Praise Him, praise Him, all ye lit - tle chil - dren,
Love Him, love Him, all ye lit - tle chil - dren,

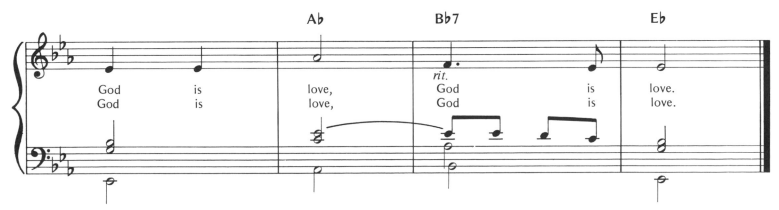

God is love, God is love.
God is love, God is love.

Softly And Tenderly Jesus Is Calling

Registration 8

Words and Music by
Will L. Thompson

Moderately slow

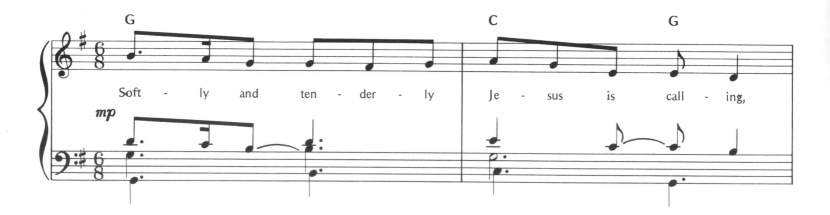

Soft - ly and ten - der - ly Je - sus is call - ing,

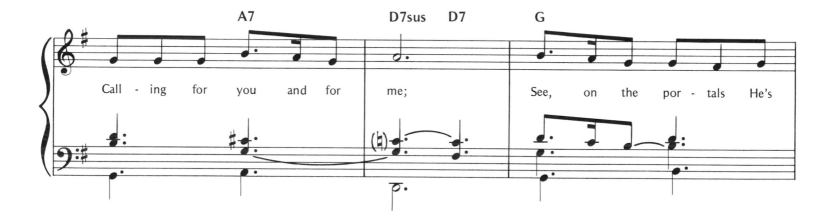

Call - ing for you and for me; See, on the por - tals He's

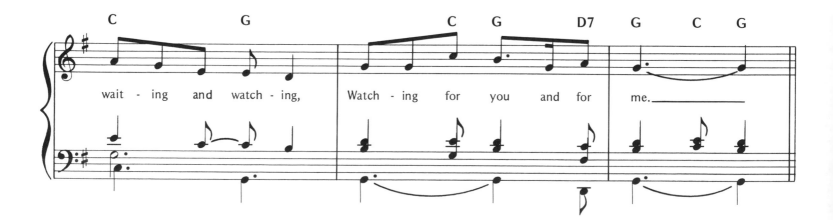

wait - ing and watch - ing, Watch - ing for you and for me.

Chorus

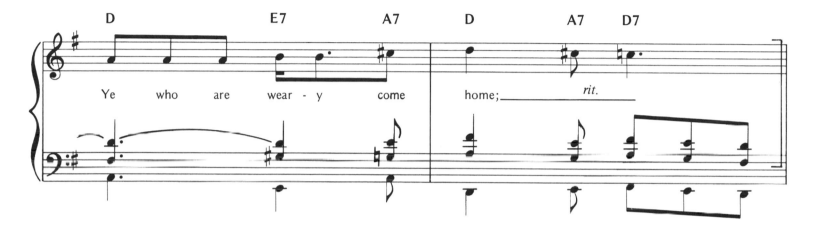

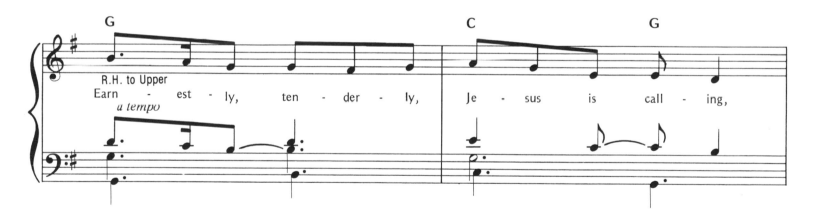

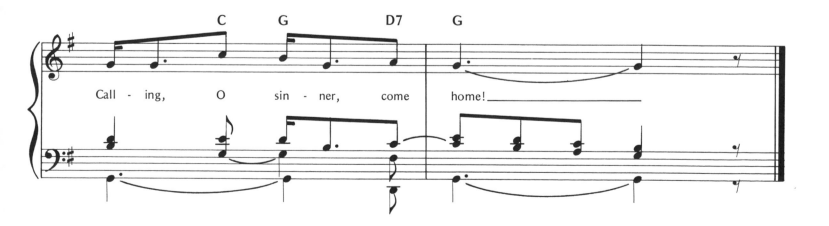

O For A Thousand Tongues To Sing

Registration 12

Words by Charles Wesley
Music by Carl G. Glaser

Moderately

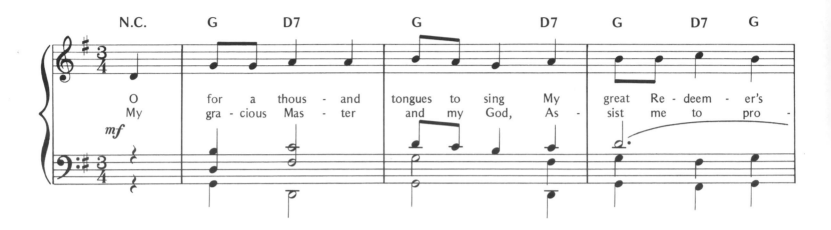

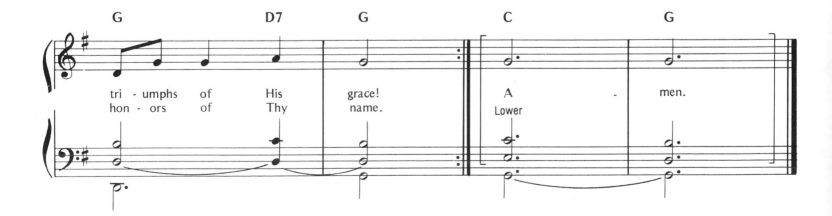

All People That On Earth Do Dwell

Registration 6

Words by William Kethe
Music by Louis Bourgeois

Moderately slow

Just A Closer Walk With Thee

Registration 15

Slowly

Music by Kenneth Morris

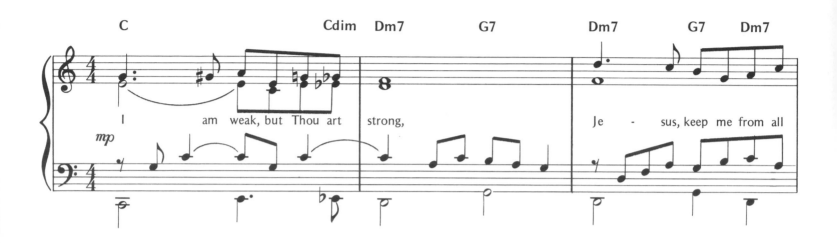

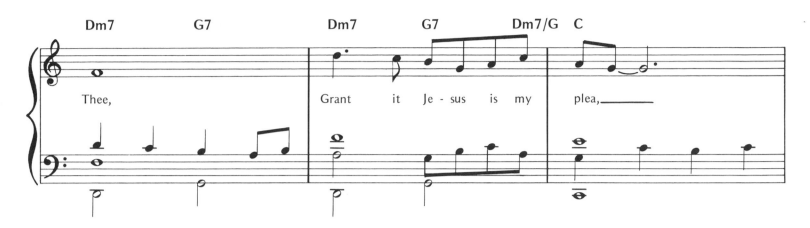

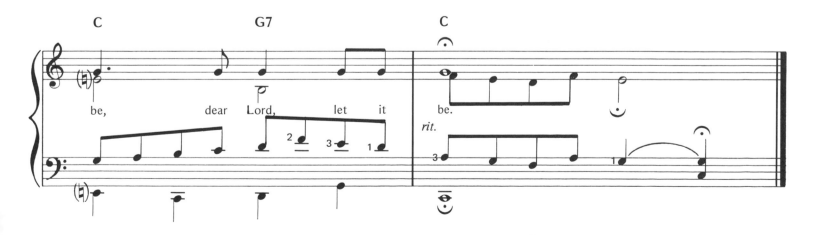

O Saviour, Precious Saviour

Registration 7

Words by Frances R. Havergal
Music by Arthur H. Mann

Out Of The Depths I Cry To Thee

Registration 3

Words from Psalm 130
Ancient German Hymn Tune

Trust And Obey

Registration 12

Words by John H. Sammis
Music by Daniel B. Towner

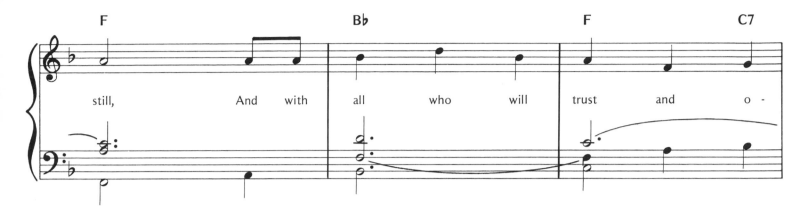

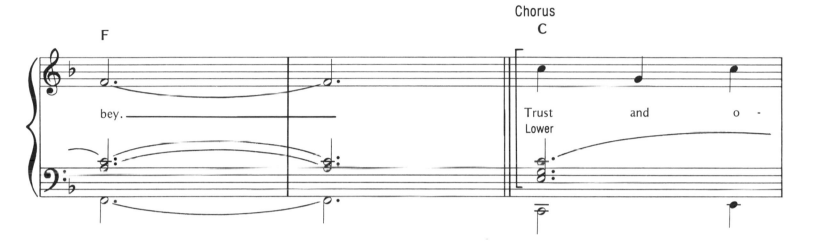

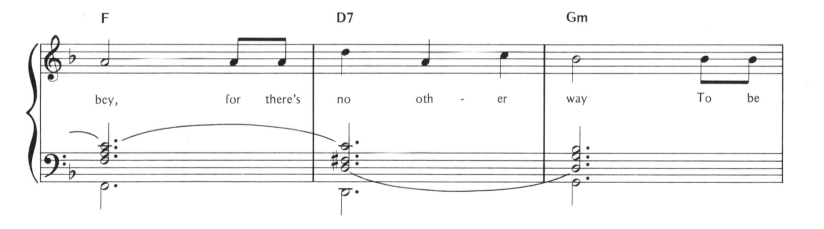

Jacob's Ladder

Registration 16

Moderately

Spiritual

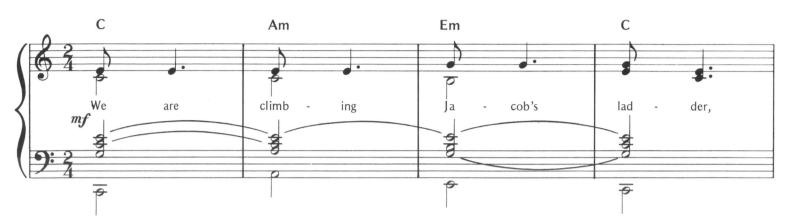

We are climb - ing Ja - cob's lad - der,

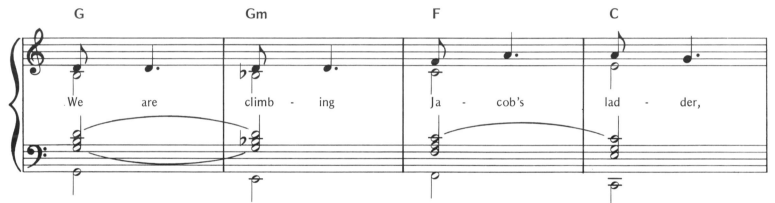

We are climb - ing Ja - cob's lad - der,

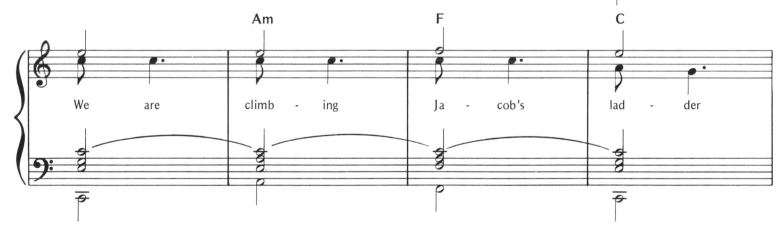

We are climb - ing Ja - cob's lad - der

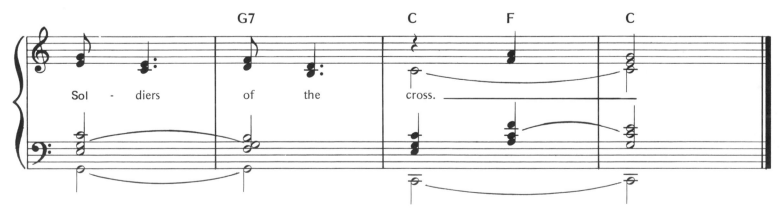

Sol - diers of the cross.

Christ Is Made The Sure Foundation

Registration 2

Words — Anonymous Latin
Music by Henry Smart

Moderately

Ah, Dearest Jesus, Holy Child

Registration 15

Words by Martin Luther
Music from "Geistliche Lieder"

Moderately

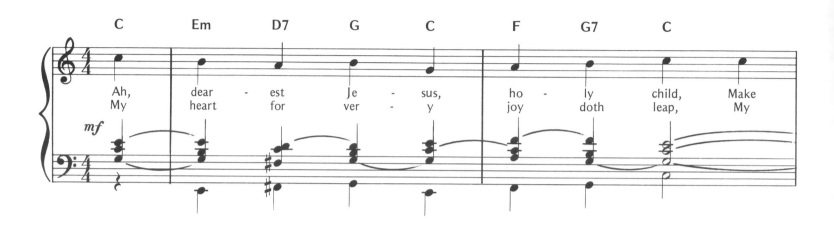

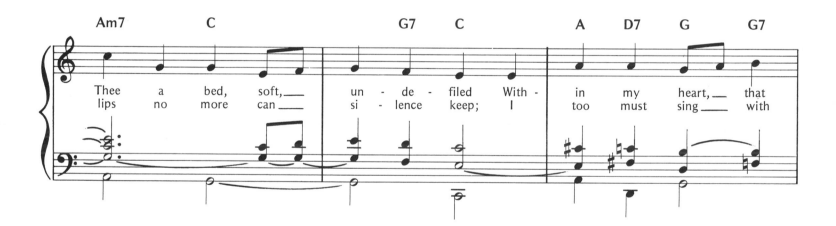

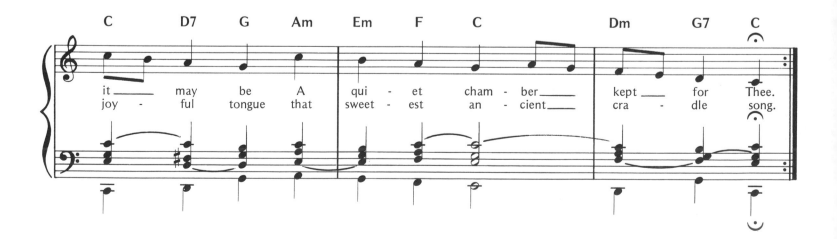

Lord, Keep Us Steadfast In Thy Word

Registration 13

Words and Music by
Martin Luther

Slowly

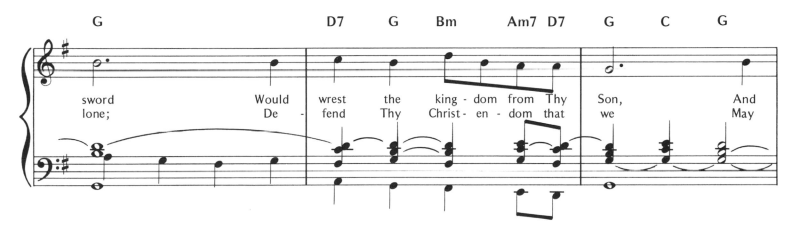

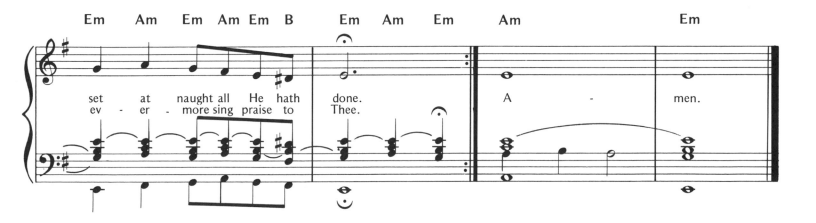

In The Sweet By And By

Registration 7

Words by S.F. Bennett
Music by Joseph P. Webster

Moderately

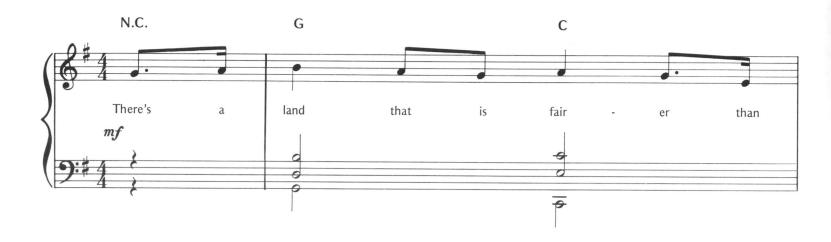

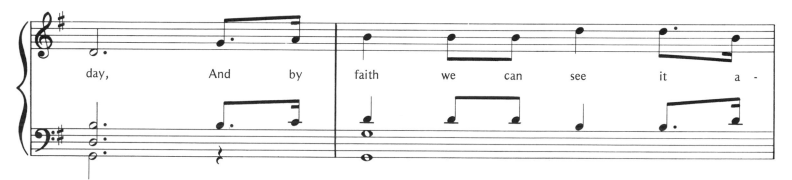

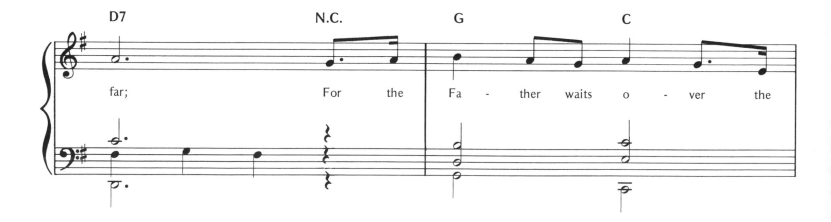

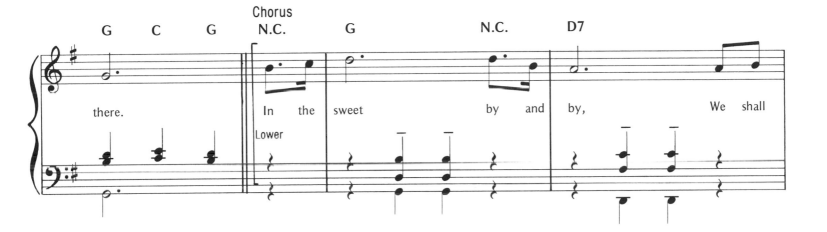

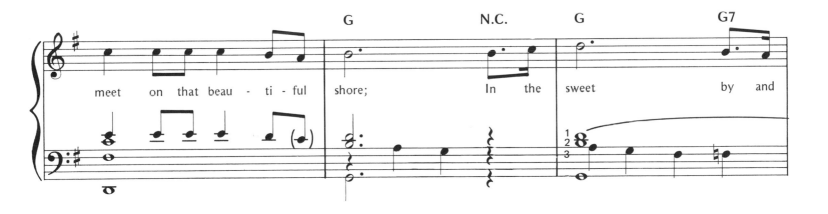

Holy God, We Praise Thy Name

Registration 3

Words by Clarence Walworth
Music from an old Austrian Hymnal

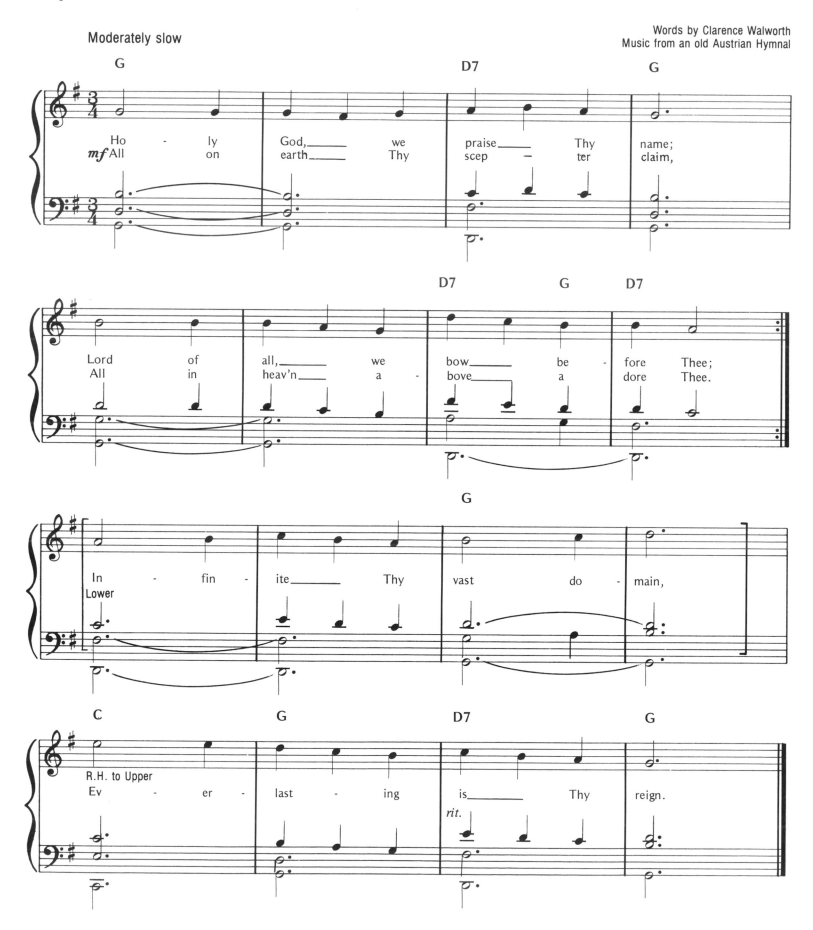

Come, Ye Thankful People, Come

Registration 19

Words by Henry Alford
Music by George J. Elvey

Moderately

Come, ye thank-ful peo-ple, come, Raise the song of har-vest home;
All is safe-ly gath-ered in, Ere the win-ter storms be-gin;
God, our Ma-ker, doth pro-vide For our wants to be sup-plied;
Lower
Come to God's own tem-ple, come, Raise the song of har-vest-home.
R.H. to Upper

For The Beauty Of The Earth

Registration 9

Words by Folliott S. Pierpoint
Music by Conrad Kocher

Only Trust Him

Registration 1

Words and Music by
John H. Stockton

Revive Us Again

Registration 11

Words by William P. Mackay
Music by John J. Husband

We praise Thee, O God! for the Son of Thy love For Je-sus who died and is now gone a-bove.

Chorus
Hal-le-lu-jah! Thine the glo-ry, Hal-le-lu-jah, A-men; Hal-le-lu-jah! Thine the glo-ry, re-vive us a-gain.

Asleep In Jesus

Registration 17

Moderately slow

Words by Margaret Mackay
Music by William B. Bradbury

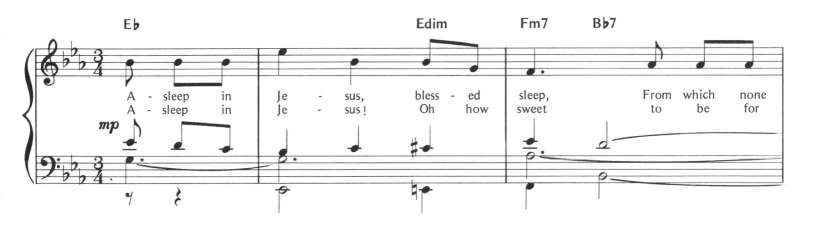

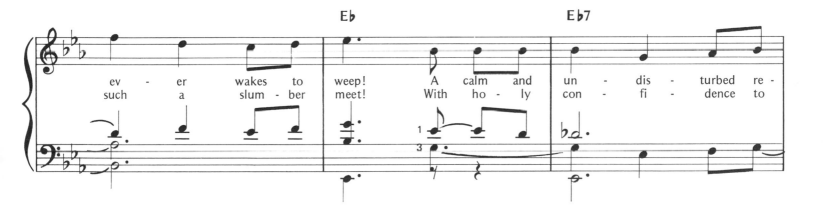

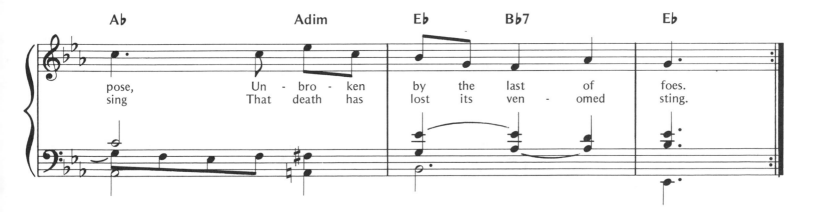

All Glory Be To God On High

Registration 1

Moderately slow

Words and Music by
Nikolaus Decius

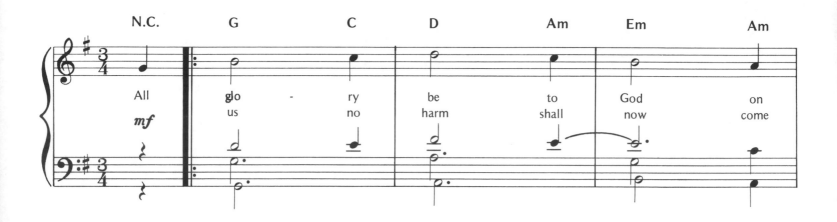

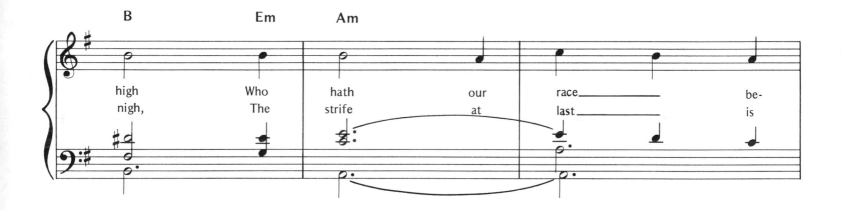

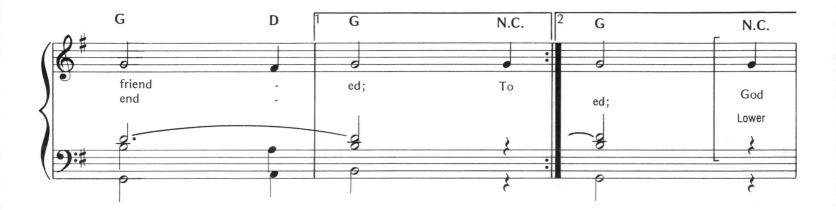

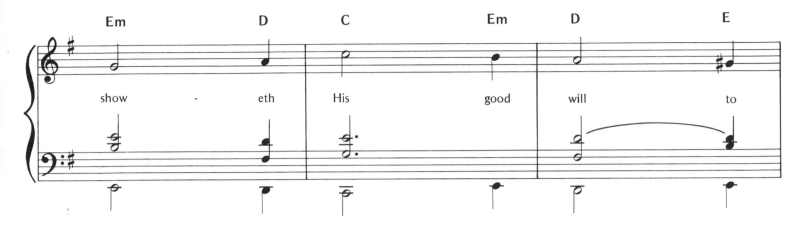

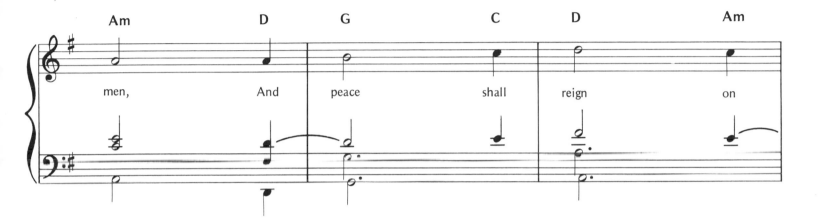

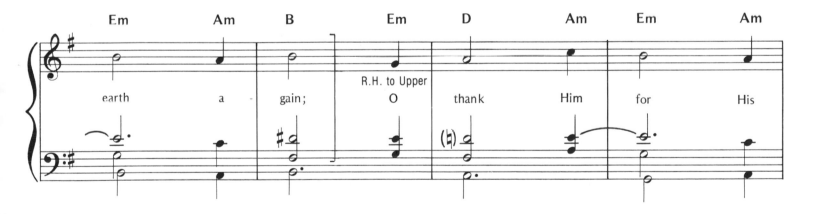

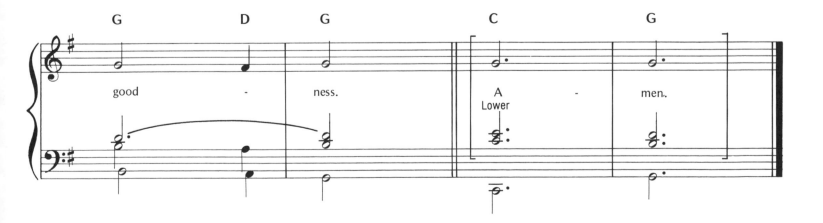

And Can It Be That I Should Gain

Registration 6

Words by Charles Wesley
Music by Thomas Campbell

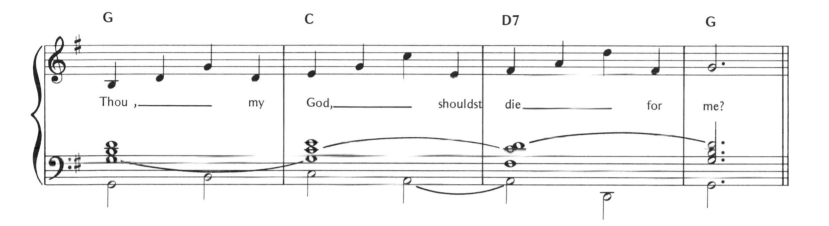

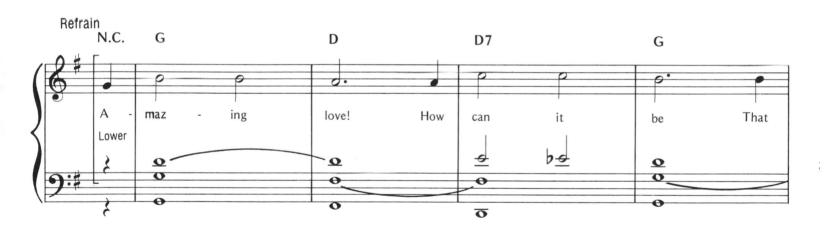

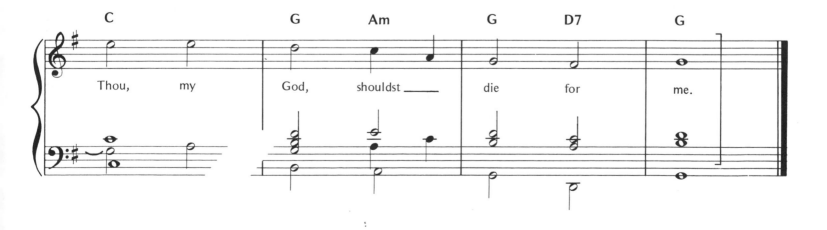

Balm In Gilead

Registration 10

Moderately (Not too fast)

Traditional Folk Melody

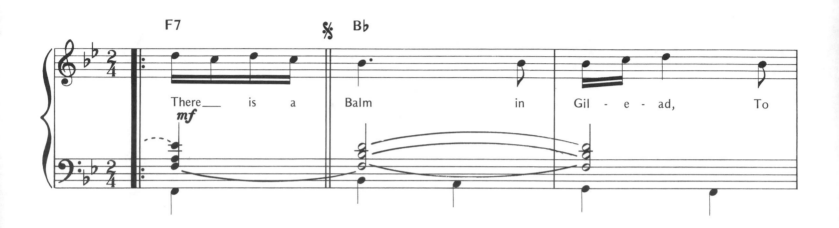

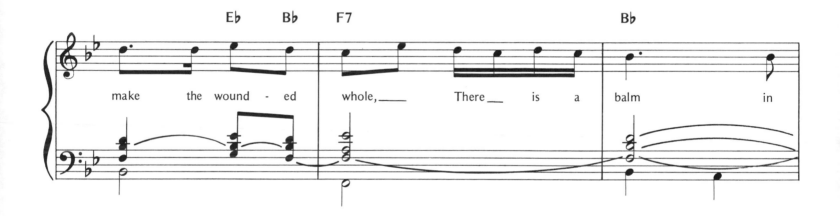

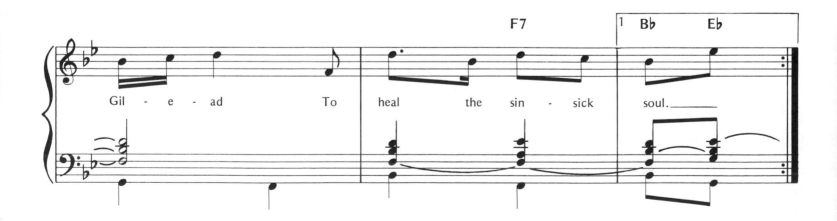

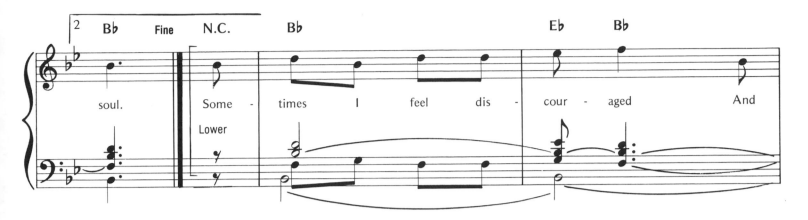

soul. Some - times I feel dis - cour - aged And
Lower

think my work's in vain, But

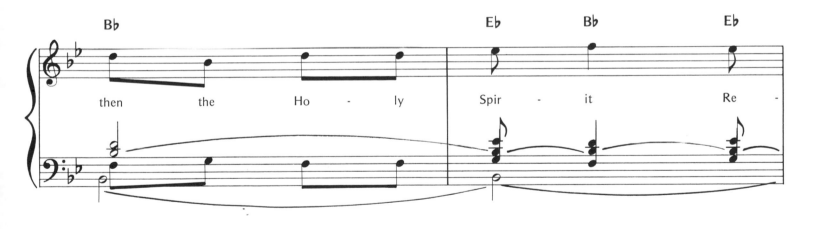

then the Ho - ly Spir - it Re -

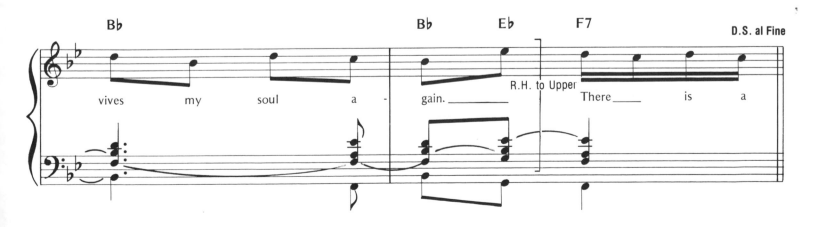

vives my soul a - gain. There____ is a

R.H. to Upper

D.S. al Fine

Blest Are The Pure In Heart

Registration 10

Moderately slow

Words by J. Keble
Music by Johann B. Konig

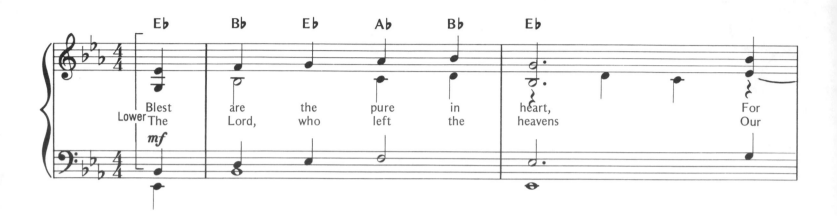

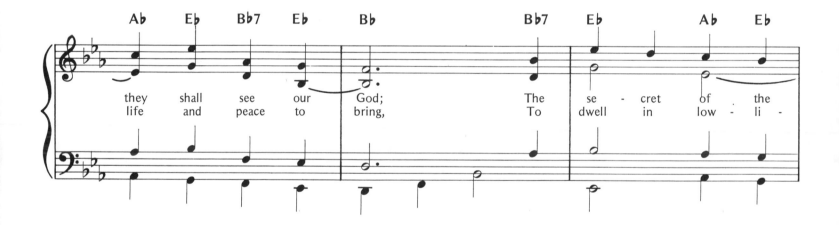

Crown Him With Many Crowns

Registration 18

Words by Matthew Bridges
Music by George J. Elvey

God Himself Is With Us

Registration 1

Words by Gerhard Tersteegen
Music by Joachim Neander

Moderately slow

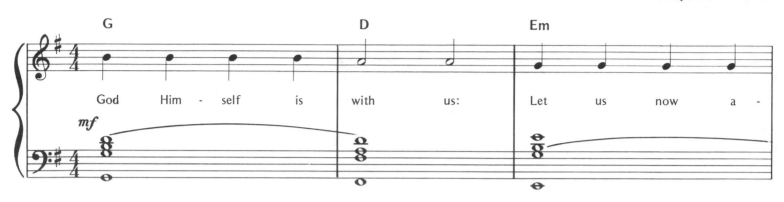

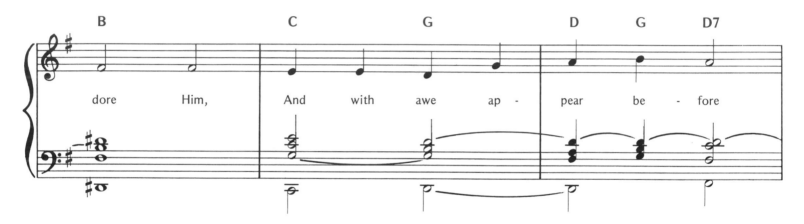

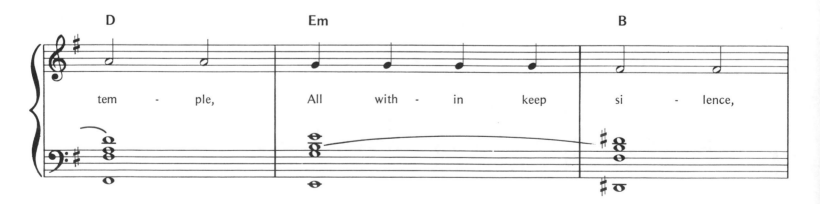

127

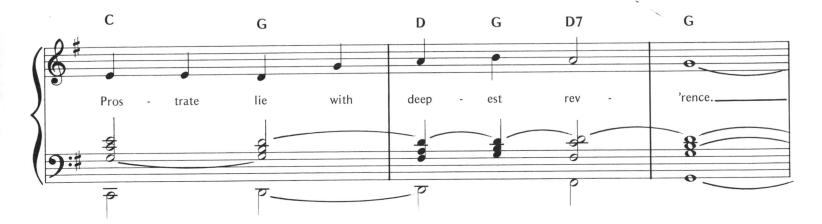

Pros - trate lie with deep - est rev - 'rence.

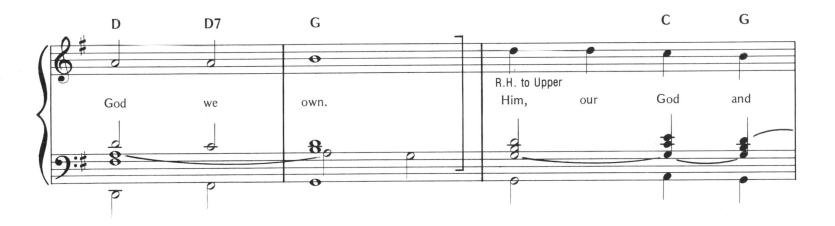

Him a - lone
Lower

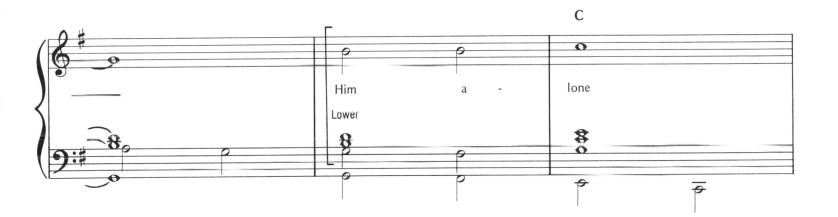

God we own.
R.H. to Upper
Him, our God and

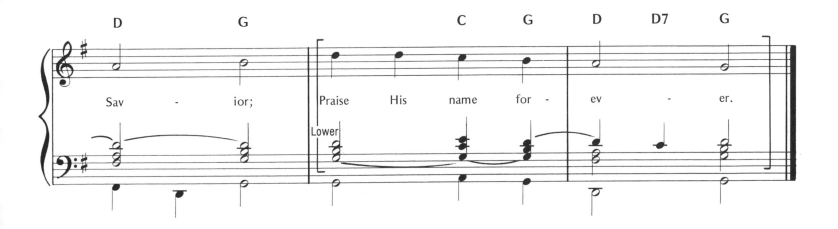

Sav - ior;
Lower
Praise His name for - ev - er.

All Nature's Works His Praise Declare

Registration 18

Made in U.S.A.

Moderately

Words by Henry Ware, Jr.
Music by Gottfried W. Fink

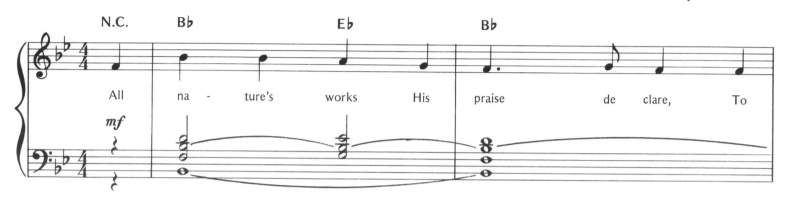

All na - ture's works His praise de clare, To

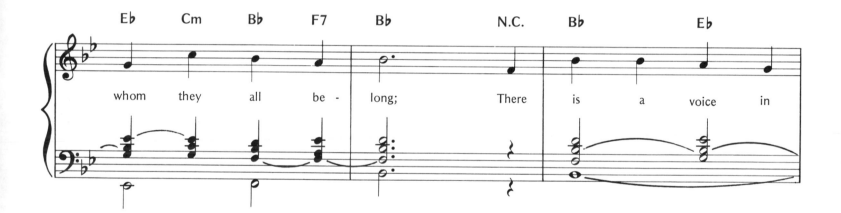

whom they all be - long; There is a voice in

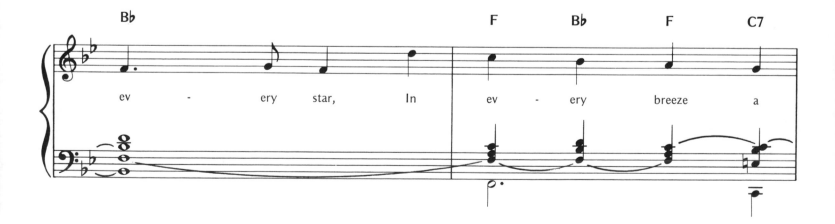

ev - ery star, In ev - ery breeze a

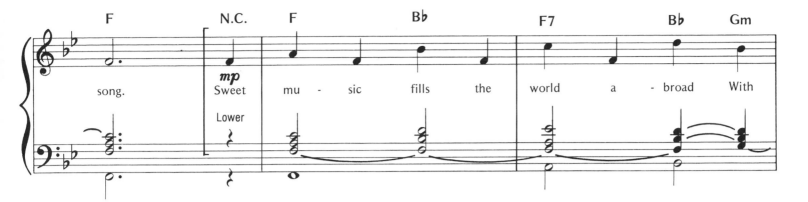

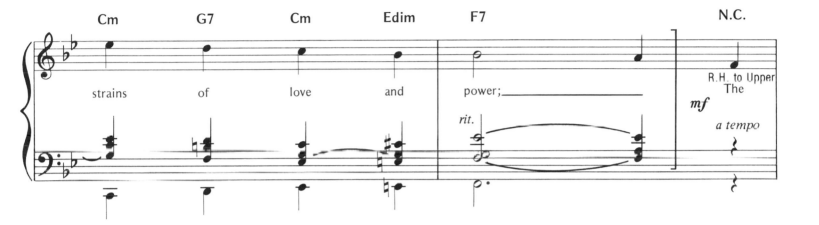

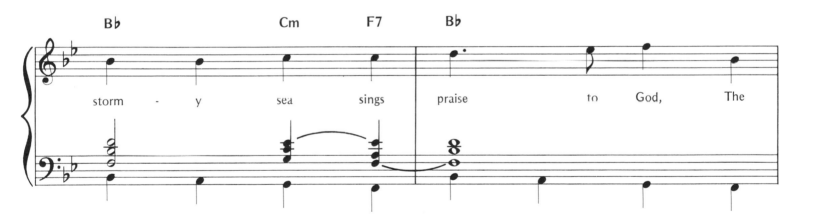

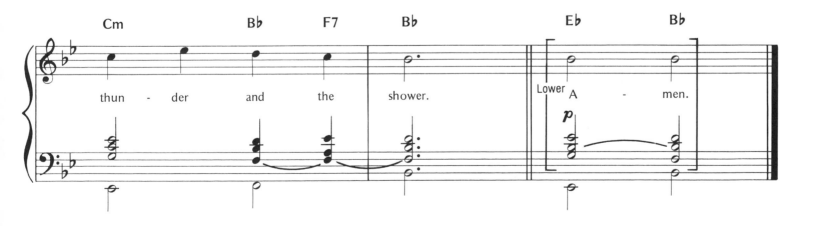

As Pants The Hart For Cooling Streams

Registration 10

Words by Psalm 42
Music by Louis Spohr

Saviour, Again To Thy Dear Name

Registration 1

Words by John Ellerton
Music by Edward J. Hopkins

Moderately

REGISTRATION CHART

Each numbered registration will produce a different sound. Match the number on the song to the same number on this chart; then engage the organ voices and controls as indicated.

1
Electronic Organs
Upper: Flute (or Tibia) 16′ (or Bassoon 16′), Reed 8′, String 4′
Lower: Flutes 8′, 4′, String 8′
Pedal: 16′, 8′ Medium Loud
Vib./Trem.: On, Full (Opt. Off)

Tonebar Organs
Upper: 88 0080 660
Lower: (00) 7755 422
Pedal: 65
Vib./Trem.: On, Full (Opt. Off)

2
Electronic Organs
Upper: Full Organ 16′, 8′, 4′, 2′, 1′ (Use Strings 8′, 4′)
Lower: Diapason 8′, Flutes 8′, 4′, 2′, String 8′, Reed 4′
Pedal: 16′, 8′ Medium Loud/Sustain
Vib./Trem.: On, Full

Tonebar Organs
Upper: 60 8586 666
Lower: (00) 7764 443
Pedal: 56 String Bass
Vib./Trem.: On, Full

3
Electronic Organs
Upper: Trumpet (or Brass) 8′
Lower: Diapason 8′
Pedal: 16′, 8′ Medium
Vib./Trem.: On, Small (Opt. Off)

Tonebar Organs
Upper: 00 6787 654
Lower: (00) 6543 221
Pedal: 53
Vib./Trem.: On, Small (Opt. Off)

4
Electronic Organs
Upper: Flutes (or Tibias) 8′, 4′, 2′, Reed 4′
Lower: Flutes 8′, 4′, Horn 8′
Pedal: 16′, 8′ Medium
Vib./Trem.: On, Full

Tonebar Organs
Upper: 00 8808 050
Lower: (00) 8880 000
Pedal: 62
Vib./Trem.: On, Full

5
Electronic Organs
Upper: Flutes (or Tibias) 8′, 4′, 2′, String 8′
Lower: Diapason 8′, Reeds 8′, 4′
Pedal: 16′, 8′ Medium Loud
Vib./Trem.: Off

Tonebar Organs
Upper: 00 8888 000
Lower: (00) 6655 554
Pedal: 55
Vib./Trem.: Off

6
Electronic Organs
Upper: Full Organ 16′, 8′, 4′, 2′, 1′ (Brilliant)
Lower: Flutes 8′, 4′, Strings 8′, 4′, Reed 4′
Pedal: 16′, 8′ Medium Loud/Sustain
Vib./Trem.: On, Full

Tonebar Organs
Upper: 60 8080 887
Lower: (00) 7754 443
Pedal: 56 String Bass
Vib./Trem.: On, Full

7
Electronic Organs
Upper: Flutes (or Tibias) 16′, 8′, 4′, 2′, 1′
Lower: Diapason 8′, Flute 8′, String 8′
Pedal: 16′, 8′ Medium
Vib./Trem.: On, Small (Opt. Off)

Tonebar Organs
Upper: 60 8808 008
Lower: (00) 6656 543
Pedal: 54
Vib./Trem.: On, Small (Opt. Off)

8
Electronic Organs
Upper: Flutes (or Tibias) 8′, 2′, String 4′, Reed 4′
Lower: Diapason 8′ (Flute 8′, String 8′)
Pedal: 16′, 8′ Medium
Vib./Trem.: Off

Tonebar Organs
Upper: 00 8008 555
Lower: (00) 6554 222
Pedal: 54
Vib./Trem.: Off

9
Electronic Organs
Upper: Flutes (or Tibias) 8′, 4′, 2′
Lower: Clarinet 8′ (or Flute 8′, Reed 4′)
Pedal: 16′, 8′ Medium
Vib./Trem.: Off

Tonebar Organs
Upper: 00 8808 000
Lower: (00) 8080 400
Pedal: 52
Vib./Trem.: Off

10
Electronic Organs
Upper: Full Organ 16′, 8′, 4′, 2′, 1′
Lower: Flutes 8′, 4′, 2′, Strings 8′, 4′
Pedal: 16′, 8′ Medium Loud
Vib./Trem.: On, Full (Opt. Off)

Tonebar Organs
Upper: 60 6666 666
Lower: (00) 7746 554
Pedal: 62
Vib./Trem.: On, Full (Opt. Off)

11
Electronic Organs
Upper: Full Organ 8′, 4′, 2′, 1′
Lower: Flute 8′, String 4′, Reed 4′
Pedal: 16′, 8′ Medium
Vib./Trem.: On, Full (Opt. Off)

Tonebar Organs
Upper: 00 8558 446
Lower: (00) 6644 232
Pedal: 55
Vib./Trem.: On, Full (Opt. Off)

12
Electronic Organs
Upper: Flute (or Tibia) 4′, Reed 8′
Lower: Diapason 8′
Pedal: 16′, 8′ Medium
Vib./Trem.: On, Small

Tonebar Organs
Upper: 00 6886 080
Lower: (00) 7633 323
Pedal: 54
Vib./Trem.: On, Small

13
Electronic Organs
Upper: String 8′
Lower: Flute 8′, Reed 4′
Pedal: 16′, 8′ Medium Soft
Vib./Trem.: On, Full (Opt. Off)

Tonebar Organs
Upper: 00 4456 667
Lower: (00) 6332 221
Pedal: 52
Vib./Trem.: On, Full (Opt. Off)

14
Electronic Organs
Upper: Flute (or Tibia) 8′, Horn 4′, String 4′
Lower: Flutes 8′, 4′
Pedal: 16′, 8′ Medium
Vib./Trem.: Off

Tonebar Organs
Upper: 00 8880 080
Lower: (00) 8800 000
Pedal: 54
Vib./Trem.: Off

15
Electronic Organs
Upper: Clarinet 8′
Lower: Flute 8′, String 4′
Pedal: 16′, 8′ Medium
Vib./Trem.: On, Full (Opt. Off)

Tonebar Organs
Upper: 00 8282 805
Lower: (00) 6543 322
Pedal: 52
Vib./Trem.: On, Full (Opt. Off)

16
Electronic Organs
Upper: Flutes (or Tibias) 8′, 4′
Lower: Flute 8′, Reed 4′
Pedal: 16′, 8′ Medium Soft
Vib./Trem.: On, Small (Opt. Off)

Tonebar Organs
Upper: 00 8008 000
Lower: (00) 6322 441
Pedal: 52
Vib./Trem.: On, Small (Opt. Off)

17
Electronic Organs
Upper: Oboe (or Reed) 8′
Lower: Flute 8′, String 4′
Pedal: 16′, 8′ Medium Soft
Vib./Trem.: Upper: Off
          Lower: On

Tonebar Organs
Upper: 00 4685 421
Lower: (00) 5433 321
Pedal: 52
Vib./Trem.: Upper: Off
          Lower: On

18
Electronic Organs
Upper: Full Organ 16′, 8′, 4′, 2′, 1′
Lower: Flutes 8′, 4′, String 8′, Reed 4′
Pedal: 16′, 8′ Medium Loud
Vib./Trem.: On, Full (Opt. Off)

Tonebar Organs
Upper: 60 8838 667
Lower: (00) 7654 332
Pedal: 65
Vib./Trem.: On, Full (Opt. Off)

19
Electronic Organs
Upper: Flutes (or Tibias) 16′, 4′, Horn 8′
Lower: Diapason 8′, String 8′
Pedal: 16′, 8′ Medium
Vib./Trem.: On, Full (Opt. Off)

Tonebar Organs
Upper: 80 0800 805
Lower: (00) 6554 221
Pedal: 54
Vib./Trem.: On, Full (Opt. Off)

20
Electronic Organs
Upper: Flutes (or Tibias) 8′, 1′, Reed 4′ (Tierce)
Lower: Flute 8′, String 4′
Pedal: 16′, 8′ Medium
Vib./Trem.: Off

Tonebar Organs
Upper: 00 8000 468
Lower: (00) 6322 222
Pedal: 54
Vib./Trem.: Off